THE VANISHING WEST

AN OVERVIEW

SIMON LENNON

The Vanishing West: An Overview
Non-Fiction (Religious Philosophy, Christian Literature and the Arts)
A book in the collection: The West
Published by Pine Hill Books
Copyright © 2020 by Simon Lennon.
All rights reserved.
This book or any portion thereof may not be reproduced, stored in or introduced into a retrieval system, or transmitted in any form or by any means whatsoever (electronic, mechanical, photocopying, recording, or otherwise) without the express written prior permission of the author and the publisher, except for the use of brief quotations in a book review, scholarly journal, or student assignment.
The author asserts his moral rights.
ISBN 978-1-925446-42-5 (electronic)
ISBN 978-1-925446-43-2 (paperback)
61,000 words
Cover image: London, 2004

In memory of my older sister

CONTENTS

Preface viii

1. Reclaiming Western Cultures 1
    Perspectives 2
    Western Civilisation 3
    Culture 4
    Cultural Heritage 6
    Cultureless Individualism 6
    Cultural Nationalism 8
    Cultural Supremacy 9
    Cultural Inferiority 9
    Assimilation 11
    Western Multiculturalism 12
    Nationalistic Multiculturalism 14
    National Identities 15
    Indigenous Cultures 16
    Traditions 17
    Festivals 18
    Postmodern Festivals 19
    Other People's Festivals 20
    Religion by Race 21
    For God and Country 23
    Death 25
    Eternity 25
    Religious Individualism 26
    Religion and War 28
    Religion and Holocaust 29
    Religious Identity 30
    The Religion of the West 31
    Religious Backgrounds and Orientations 32
    Christianity and Rights 33
    Christianity and Science 34
    Cultural Christianity 36
    Christian Countries 37
    Cultural Revisionism 38
    Historical Revisionism 39
    Owning Culture 40

Cultural Appropriation 41
Haute Couture 43
Artistic Nationalism 44
Artistic Relativism 45
Multicultural Arts 46
Art 47
Sculpture 48
Architecture and Design 49
Homes and Houses 51
Décor and Fashion 51
Prose 52
Poetry 54
Songs 55
Music 56
Dance 57
Celebrity 57
Theatre 58
Films 59
The Solace of Television 60
Television Themes 62
The Broken West 63
Saving the West 64
Censorship 65
The Future 66

2. Christendom Lost 68

Western Christianity 68
Christian Individualism 69
Belonging 71
Social Justice 71
Asylum Seekers 72
Biblical Races 73
Biblical Nations 75
Jewish Guilt 76
Western Guilt 76
The Church and the Holocaust 78
Feeling Unforgiven 79
Self-Sacrifice 80
Infant Baptism 81
Christian Upbringing 82

Mixed Marriages 83
Natural Morality 84
Western Immorality 85
Postmodern Christianity 86
Multicultural Christianity 87
Christ-less Christianity 89
Religious Nihilism 90
Other Races' Christianity 91
The Nature of God 92
The Race of Jesus 94
The White Christian Burden 95
Saving Everyone Else 97
Other People's Churches 98
Church and State 99
Secularity 101
Oaths and Pledges 102
Christian Education 103
Atheism and Agnosticism 104
Religion at Work 105
Economic Religion 106
Spirituality 107
Sport 109
A Multicultural Inquisition 111
The Religion that Hides 112
Our Lands of Other Faiths 114
Karma 115
Holy Mothers 116
Armageddon 117
Conservation 117
Environmentalism 118
Climate Change 120
Voluntary Western Extinction 121
Voluntary Human Extinction 122
Christian Faith 124
The Crusades 125
Christian Walls 126
Christian Nationalism 126

3. Aiding Islam 128

Imperial Turkey 129

Islamisation	131
The End of the Cold War	132
Serbia	133
Multiculturalism at War	135
The Iron Boot of Multiculturalism	137
Other People's Wars	138
For Other People's God and Country	139
September Eleven, 2001	140
War without Enemies	142
The War That Is Not	143
The Religion of Peace	145
Losing their Religion	146
Religious Conviction	147
Funding Islam	148
Causes of Terror	149
Staving off Prejudice	150
Wartime Propaganda	152
Abandoning Our Vulnerable	153
Coexistence	154
Islamophobia	155
Hate Crimes	157
Muslims as Jews	159
Freedom from Speech	160
Muslim Nationalism	161
Islamic Altruism	162
Solidarity with Muslims	163
Joining Islam	164
Terrorist Rights	165
Bad Christians	167
Love and Terror	168
The Peace of Individuals	170
The Peace of Nations	171
Islamic Land	173
Religious Replacement	174
Anti-Semitism	175
Sharia	176
The Islamisation of the West	177
Our Lands of Other People	179
About the Author	182

PREFACE

White people are rejecting our cultures and heritage while eagerly adopting other races' cultures and heritages, as no other race could imagine. We are erasing ourselves and our forebears, at the expense of our descendants.

Examining how we came to this extraordinary situation and its implications is my collection of eleven non-fiction books titled *The West*, comprising four series of two or three books each: *Individualism*, *Identity*, *Nationalism*, and *Cultures*. This overview, *The Vanishing West*, collates into a single volume the principal ideas from the fourth series, *Cultures*, comprising:

1. *Reclaiming Western Cultures*.
2. *Christendom Lost*.
3. *Aiding Islam*.

Reclaiming Western Cultures and *Christendom Lost* are essentially the same books. The former caters to readers without Christian faith. The latter caters to readers claiming Christian faith.

Three companion overviews, *The Unnatural West*, *The Tribeless West*, and *The Homeless West* collate into single volumes the principal ideas from the first three series: *Individualism*, *Identity*, and *Nationalism*. Being unnaturally tribeless, the homeless West is vanishing.

Vanishing in the way we are is unnatural. Because we have become unnatural, the West is vanishing.

These overviews omit the foundations, evidence, and examples supporting those ideas, for which readers so interested may turn to those eleven books and their bibliographies. Generally, those foundations, evidence, and examples are in the book described by the chapter in which those ideas appear. For ease of reading and understanding, some ideas appear in other chapters of this overview and its companion overviews.

Much as the Far East means East Asian races, their cultures, and civilisations and the Middle East means Arabs, Jews, and their cultures and civilisations, so does the West mean peoples racially

European, our cultures and civilisation. Whether Europeans are one race or several races and the West is one civilisation or several civilisations, such as Scottish, Welsh, Irish, and so forth, is a matter of nomenclature, as it is for other races and ethnicities. We could be said to be different European races but the same Western Civilisation.

Westerners are white people. People hostile to the West are hostile to white people, and vice versa. People defending one defend the other.

Please consider the ideas in this overview and the books. If the West is going to progress from this Age of Ideology to a New Age of Enlightenment, an Age of Re-Enlightenment, back to reason, morality, and the pursuit of truth, we are going to have to learn again to consider ideas new to us. We will need again to discuss matters rationally with each other.

1. RECLAIMING WESTERN CULTURES

Individualism remains central to the decline of the West, not the least because it leaves us indifferent to that decline: to the fate of our race, culture, and civilisation of which we no longer feel we are part. Understanding white people in the early twenty-first century requires recognising our disregard for each other, our forebears, and our descendants, whatever our reason.

We might presume that our particular lives do not affect our family and race. They do.

We might be advancing or simply saving our careers, which depend upon our disinterest in our family and race. Those careers might be academic, journalistic, or increasingly anything else.

We might want more money, as we in the West do. We might want votes.

We might think that the end of the West will broaden the music on offer, or widen our choice of cuisine. It will not, on either score.

Worse than our indifference, is our animosity. Without belief in Western Civilisation, we might yearn for something else in which to believe. Decades of deceit will have convinced us that ruining our race, or replacing our race with other races, is a cause worth pursuing. It is not.

Needing to feel part of something, we might echo other people's hostility to our race. Resisting that hostility feels difficult, but it is, or will become, towards us.

As wicked as the worst of us are white people motivated not by money, music, or menus, let alone despair, loneliness, or timidity, but by their sanctimonious self-righteousness. The most ruthlessly self-serving of individuals, they revel in the adoration they think they receive from the races they advance. They signal their supposed virtues to people privately holding them in contempt, even hating them.

Money passing between them does not diminish those other races' contempt. Money accentuates contempt.

Being individuals, we care little for what does not affect us in our lifetimes, provided that we have the friends we want, maintain our ideologies of inclusion, and assure our little selves we are good. The immorality of individualism is never more in evidence than in our willingness and even enthusiasm to let our race, cultures, and civilisation vanish.

People consumed by their individualism might not care about saving their race, country, and culture until they realise the benefits that their race, country, and culture are to them. The changes arising will only bother them if those changes affect them personally, before they die in their solitary space where no one can hear them. They care even less what happens afterwards.

Caring about the benefits of Western races, cultures, and civilisation to other people, including our descendants, requires morality. Instead, we are individuals.

Perspectives

Most peoples' views of the world cannot help but be from their perspectives. A people's perspective is more than two eyes alone ever see.

Increasingly since the Second World War, Western education systems have come to teach history (and progressively everything else) from the perspectives not of the West but of other races. We do not learn our forebears' perspectives.

Seeing World War II through Jewish eyes, the Jewish view of our forebears and us became our view. We feel what Jews feel, looking back through the thick prism of Holocaust.

Aside from Jews through the Holocaust, we do not learn the perspectives of other races' forebears. We learn perspectives of other races today. Feeling their forebears suffered at our forebears' hands suits them, much as feeling they suffer at our hands today suits them.

As it is supposed to do, immigration prevents us from celebrating our history, honouring our dead. Endless sensitivity to other races may well be cathartic, but encouraging them to hate us, neglecting the truth, the result is never anything of which we can be proud.

Other races' histories are not a problem. A rare distraction from our economic lives is hearing of other people's pasts, tainted with tales against us.

While we forever look at everything from other races' perspectives, the only perspectives of which we are unaware are our own, but ultimately, no person can ever really have a perspective but his or her own. No race can have a perspective but its own. Individualism, multiculturalism, and other diversity are our new Western perspectives.

No wonder Western education systems lag behind education systems in Asia. While Western school curricula focus on equality and other races' perspectives, East Asians focus upon excellence and their races' perspectives.

Our view is no less Eurocentric for being our disdain for ourselves and our forebears, cloaked in our deprecation. We rarely look back to discover how recently we changed, or the reason we changed.

Western Civilisation

While continuing to better ourselves, our forebears knew our civilisation to be fundamentally the best for us. Presuming our civilisation was also best for other races underpinned Roman, Napoleonic, and other European imperialism.

Western Civilisation we shared with the world was more than grand buildings and architecture, governments and administration, art and music. Civilisation of any nature encompasses people connecting or in some way co-operating with each other. It requires people to identify with each other in a common, functioning structure.

Instead, through the twentieth century, we became individuals. Western individualism, as it has come to be, is intrinsically incompatible with civilisation.

We co-operate with each other to the extent there is money involved, but that does not make us a civilisation. It makes us an economy.

Early in the twenty-first century, we reject more than our forebears' imperialism. We refuse to defend any part of our forebears' civilisation.

Part of our problem is that the West, namely European races and any sense of the lands and cultures that we possess, is a racist concept. Thus Western Civilisation and Western anything else are racist concepts.

Racism has come to include linking any thought, taste, or action to a race. Peoples of the world are supposed to speak with the same voice and be so much the same, in all the same ways. Alternatively, each person is supposed to be unique, in every way. When we categorise people, we cannot do so by race or religion.

With tribe or race, civilisation might develop. Without a collective identity, there is no civilisation.

Equally racist are all other races and their civilisations: the Middle East, the Far East, and more, with their constituent races and civilisations such as Chinese and Japanese. Egyptian and other ancient civilisations were also racist.

We are not worried about that racism, not since the Holocaust. Neither, for the most part, is anyone else.

If Western Civilisation is a misnomer, it is because each European race enjoyed its own civilisation. If Western Civilisation was not a single civilisation, then it describes the features that different European civilisations shared.

Denying there is a West or Western Civilisation without denying other races their races and civilisations is a tactic of those who would eradicate us. What they do not denigrate, they deny.

Denying there are any races or civilisations is a tactic of those who would eradicate everyone. Globalism tries to build the world anew, with a universal order around ideology and economics, but there will never be a global civilisation as the West understands civilisation to be. The rest of the world does not want it.

The rest of the world retains its tribes, races, and nations. They are not as interested as we are in ideologies. They have more than their economies. They have religion and other culture.

If there ever is a world civilisation, then it will be because an imperial race or league of races imposes its civilisation upon everyone else. Rights, religion, and everything else will be for that race or league, not us or anyone else, to determine.

Culture

One aspect of civilisation, culture is everything that people think and do beyond the mere mechanics of life: their activities and attitudes. Thus culture includes styles of houses, clothes, and food beyond the plainest necessities of shelter and sustenance.

Other races know what their cultures are, without feeling a need to particularise them. We know their cultures too, without knowing the details.

Ours are the cultures we no longer recall. To talk of Western cultures, we founder, not altogether sure what culture means anymore or what our cultures were.

When we think of culture, we tend to think of food and beverage characteristic of a race, without thinking of race. Our only certainty is that culture encompasses eating other people's food and drinking anyone's beverage.

What were Western cultures disappear into multicultural monotony. The essence is all much the same: we feast on immigrant foods. Only the bills of fare change.

Multiculturalism becomes no culture, aside from eating and drinking. We of the West are not the only people to enjoy food and drink. We are the only people to dwell so much upon them. Eating and drinking take up inordinate proportions of our lives and feelings.

We laugh at the food of our forebears, but if we had the self-respect that other races enjoy, we would respect our cuisines more than we do. We would enjoy them again.

England had much more food than meat pies, fish and chips, and Yorkshire pudding, however satisfying they were. Scotland had more beverage than beer, whisky, and cider, however pleasing they were. Our food and beverage were whatever enough of us made and consumed that most of the world did not.

Culture is much, much more than just food and beverage. Our cultures comprised all that cultures can be, for good and for bad. Our problem is: we have come to feel only the bad.

The only thing worse than the contempt that kills so much of our cultures, is the conceit that imagines other races maintaining the morsels we like. We cannot expect other races to continue our cultural heritage when we do not continue it. If we do not rediscover our heritage and reclaim it for us, nobody else will sustain it.

Cultures cannot exist without people to practice and possess them; our cultures cannot survive us. In every respect, we are the vanishing West.

Cultural Heritage

Our forebears developed our cultures because our cultures expressed and reflected us. Other cultures did not. England had pretty peaceful gardens much softer than those in Japan, villages with fêtes and bring-and-buy sales. Our races and cultures served us well, which we forgot through two world wars and a holocaust.

Immigrant parents want their children to learn their cultural heritage (the good aspects anyway). Trying hard to make multiculturalism work, we want our children to learn other races' cultural heritage too.

We cannot imagine our children learning our cultural heritage. Western cultures defy what we are trying to achieve: our new model earth.

If we are not presuming our past was a time of an ugly one culture, we are presuming we had no culture at all. What remains of Western history and heritage is what remains of the West: politics and economics. Once in a while, our children put aside hearing how awful we were.

Only in the West is a patriotic school curriculum controversial, although curricula do not need to be patriotic to be filled with Western arts and culture, amidst the achievements of Western Civilisation. They need only to be honest, focused upon excellence.

Multiculturalism depends upon our children's ignorance of the cultures they are losing. If they fairly knew of their heritage, they would pursue more knowledge about it. They would reclaim it.

Any education system is woefully incomplete if it does not teach children their culture and history. There might be value in knowing something of other cultures because there might be value in better understanding other races, but that depends upon us knowing the facts about other races as best we can, instead of what they claim the facts were.

That also depends upon us understanding our cultures beforehand. The more we learn of other races in our finite lives on earth, the less we learn of ourselves. We do not know anything.

Cultureless Individualism

There is a wealth of our cultural inheritance we rarely notice around us. If we do notice it, we do not consider it ours.

Culture is a collective expression of beliefs and behaviours recurrent among a people but not the rest of the world. Of itself, culture does not depend upon people co-operating with each other. It does depend upon a common, collective identity.

Estranged from each other, individuals fail to recognise our cultures because we cannot sense the races or other collective identities of which we are part. Without racism, individuals do not feel a cultural legacy to inherit, possess, and develop, let alone to defend and pass onto their descendants. Cultures are racist.

Premised upon our postmodern individualism, we have only our single-person lifestyles. We have only our personal beliefs, arts, and crafts.

Implicit in cultures are stereotypes, but we have become fussed about stereotypes defying our individualism. Other people's lifestyles are not ours to notice, unless we feel they affect us. In terms of our relations with others, there are only economics and ideology, as the West has become.

Communists obsessed with the mechanics of life. Neglecting culture meant that accommodation, clothes, and food became bland.

People dying, homeless, and starving are of necessity fixated with the mechanics of life. The rich West does not need to be so fixated, but only commerce and the world it creates survive. We are not even looking for the cultures that could have been ours.

While Western countries no longer claim to have cultures, we respect other races having cultures, even civilisations, because we respect their racial and other collective identities. Poor races around the world find more time for their cultures than many of us prospering in the West find for ours.

Commerce and ideologies conceal us. Companies so cavalier about immigration can lose money from the loss of our cultures, although they are careful not to complain. Complaining would be racist, even where there is money at stake.

Cultures reveal us, because they reveal our race. Only peoples have cultures, heritages, and thus cultural heritages.

For us to recover our cultures, we need to recognise we are races. Connecting us to our race connects us to our cultures: fine craftwork by people we do not know, paintings by artists who have died. For us to salvage our civilisation, we need to feel we are nations.

Cultural Nationalism

We think the world is becoming Western because we see suits and shops in other people's cities, American films in their cinemas, and rich emirs buying our art, but Western cultures never denied us cheap meals in other people's restaurants or rubbishy Japanese films, from time to time. Other races watch and eat what we produce that they like, if only for the course of a fad. They do not feel the passion for everything Western that we feel for everything not. Nor need they feel it.

With their racial and other collective identities, they possess their cultures. Retaining the self-respect that we lost through the twentieth century, races other than ours value their cultures, if only for the benefit their culture provide them. Cultural and other nationalism is premised upon self-belief.

Most countries outside the West enjoy cultural and racial homogeneity. They maintain their purity, content to be left in their peace.

While we criticise what smidgeons remain of Western cultures, we admire other countries retaining their cultural homogeneity. We do not call them backward, bland, or insular as we describe our past homogeneity. We do not criticise their monocultures, traditions, and values. We holiday there.

Monocultures need not be stagnant. They are chances to evolve upon a people's terms, becoming what they wish to become.

Safe in their countries of origin, other races take what they like from other cultures, without besmirching their culture, much as we used to do. They refuse the rest.

Meanwhile, their émigrés in the vanishing West remain defiantly bound to keep what they have. We imagine multiculturalism promoting positive change within immigrant communities. Instead, keeping their affinity to their ancestral lands, multiculturalism pressures them to hold fast to their traditional cultures. What was supposed to change became changelessness, among immigrants.

It is a fascinating irony. Cultures evolve among the confidence of monocultural security more than amidst the competitiveness of cruel multiculturalism.

Cultural Supremacy

The Arab, Asian, and other cultures we are so keen to foster in the West are already in the Middle East, Asia, and so forth. Ours are not, in any meaningful way. Nor will they be, among people respecting their races and cultures.

Races other than ours like their cultures dominating countries, be those countries theirs or not. They naturally prefer their cultures to anyone else's culture.

They might consider themselves racially and culturally superior to everyone else. They might consider themselves racially and culturally superior only to some other races and cultures. They might simply retain their senses of race and culture.

If their countries are not completely reserved to their races and cultures, their races and cultures predominate in their countries. In every region and country outside the West, a race and its culture dominates, even where there are minority races and cultures. Being its country entitles a race to its cultural supremacy, whatever other races live there.

Were white people to imagine the same for Western countries, we would be called white supremacists, as if that were a fault. White supremacy has become any sense that our race and cultures should dominate Western countries, in the way that other races and cultures dominate their countries.

Neither they nor we complain of Japanese supremacy in Japan, African supremacy in Africa, or any other racial and cultural supremacy outside the West. If comment about other races' supremacy in their countries seems ludicrous, then so are complaints of white supremacy in Western countries.

If we laughed off complaints of white supremacy in the West instead of apologising for whatever remains of our cultures, trying to undo them, those complaints might drop away. White supremacy becomes any sense that our race, cultures, and civilisation should survive.

Cultural Inferiority

Other races refuse to oblige. The West obliges. Valuing our races and cultures is racist, as it is not for people of other races.

Rather than refuse other races and risk conflict between us, we erase what remains of our cultures and civilisation, in countries we agree we should not dominate: countries no longer ours. We call it multiculturalism.

Multiculturalism expresses the West's determination to embrace other races and religions that began with our embracing of Jews after the Holocaust. Instead of our cultures, we value multiculturalism, but multiculturalism is not a culture or collection of cultures. It is an ideology.

The lack of a dominant culture is at the core of Western countries' problems, although some cultures dominating are worse than none dominating. Our trouble is: we think our cultures are among them.

In our weak Western eyes, cultural relativism makes no culture, especially ours, preferable to any other. However other races behave, we refuse to consider any culture primitive or barbaric, except our own.

Multiculturalism is another ideology premised upon our lack of self-belief, if not self-contempt. Acknowledging there could be multiculturalism requires recognition of differences between cultures. Embracing multiculturalism requires the sense that our cultures alone were inadequate.

Admiring, enjoying, or appreciating the arts and cultures of another race can be reasonable, when it is done on their merits, aesthetics, or other appeal. Other races do.

Our failing is that we admire, enjoy, and appreciate the arts and cultures of other races for no other reason than that they are the arts and cultures of other races. Being of other races means they appeal to us. Merit and aesthetics do not enter into it.

Of all the cultures jostling about, the only cultures unvalued are ours. We do not value culture we know to be ours, because it is ours. Culture we like, we do not consider ours.

When we celebrate the coming of multiculturalism, we celebrate other people's cultures. When we talk of other cultures enriching us, we call our cultures poor by comparison, but immigrants have not enriched our cultures because our cultures were rich before they came.

If we wanted to be generous to other races and if we focus only upon the good of all cultures, then we could say that every culture has riches. Refusing to recognise that some cultures are richer than others is lazy.

No cultures have been richer than the classic cultures of Europe. Especially in Europe, we lost sense of how rich they were.

By the twenty-first century, much of our cultures are passé, as other people's cultures are not. If anybody asks what we want, the only answer we dare give is more multiculturalism, without thought of our cultures.

All we celebrate is other races and their cultures. We think we would be failures without them.

We keep on kotowing to other races in the name of respect without respecting ourselves, as if there is nothing in us or our cultures to respect. Without us respecting ourselves, other races do not respect us or our cultures. If we did respect ourselves, there would be no multiculturalism.

Assimilation

When immigrants from other races were rare, and the only reasons they had to come and to stay were us and our cultures, many in large part assimilated with us. Through the twentieth century, we welcomed them en masse.

Throughout the West, we initially assumed that immigrants from other races would join us in our lifestyles, much as immigrants from our particular races assimilated with us. To think immigrants from other races would not assimilate with us would be to admit differences between races, when racism had come to seem wrong.

Immigrants no longer came for us or our cultures, but for money and other benefits we provided them: the mechanics of life. They had no need culturally to assimilate.

Nevertheless, we continue to assume immigrants from other races will become like us because past European immigrants became like us, but past European immigrants were already like us before they arrived. Other races were not.

We do not notice immigrants not adopting our cultures, because we have no sense of what our cultures are, or were. We see immigrants in the shops and supermarkets so are certain they assimilate, while we buy the foods that they buy.

The only assimilation is among immigrants from countries and cultures already like those of their hosts: immigrants from the same race. When aspects of different cultures assimilate, then it is because those aspects were already alike. Immigrants assimilate to that extent, without needing to change. Even fellow Europeans, once their numbers become large enough, do not assimilate with us any more than they were already like us before they arrived.

Whether they are immigrant or indigenous, people of other races but ours consider assimilation into any other culture to be denying them their rights to live as they please. They are right, if we think there is a right for people to live by their cultures, but that is not a right we keep for ourselves.

Assimilation having failed across races and across ethnic groups within races, interracial immigration demands multiculturalism. Other races do not need to accommodate us when we accommodate them, but maintaining any kind of culture is hard when we accommodate everyone else, without thought of our cultures.

When Western values and the rest of our cultures conflict with those of other races, other races do not defer to our cultures. We defer to theirs, because those cultures are theirs.

With immigrants refusing to adopt our ways, we adopt theirs. Rather than immigrants assimilating with us, we assimilate with them, in our desperate desire to make immigration work.

We have given other races the right to maintain their lifestyles without retaining that right for ourselves. Abandoning ourselves to our immigrants rather than asking anything of them, we have little left to retain, little to get in the way. We struggle whenever we try.

We do not imagine Britain's problems, or the problems of other Western countries, nowadays being due to mass immigration. Instead, we blame our problems upon us trying to save something of being British: of being ourselves.

Losing our homelands means losing not just our races, but also our cultures and civilisation. If we do not presume that our races and cultures will survive interracial immigration, we hope they do not.

Western Multiculturalism

We call our countries multicultural, but ours is Western

multiculturalism. In our determination to make our countries those of every culture, we lose our cultures.

At best, we refuse to allow any culture priority over another; we do not want one race offending another. No people are expected to predominate, especially not us.

Reducing cultures to the least of them leaves none of them worthwhile: cultural nihilism. We beg other races not to buy into our cultures and insist that our race not remain in, letting their cultures deny us our cultures until our cultures have gone. Far from building anything new, we are simply losing the old.

Western countries become cultureless, because we are determined that cultures not impinge upon each other. Our vision of a world without countries becomes a world without cultures, as it was with communism.

Western multiculturalism is premised upon globalism: our rejection of nations. The essence of Western multiculturalism is that we are discarding our countries and cultures.

Other races do not share our cultureless vision. Just as well the rest of the world keeps its countries and cultures. If they adopted Western multiculturalism, there would be sameness and soullessness the world over.

At worst, Western multiculturalism promotes other cultures at the expense of ours. Unwinding our cultures from our countries as best as we can, multiculturalism is the framework by which other cultures fill the void left behind.

If we have cultures, those cultures are no longer ours. Multiculturalism leaves us overwhelmed by people who believe in themselves and their culture.

Multiculturalism has become another ideology the foes of Western peoples wield against us. Condemned for being the so-called culture wars were not the multiculturalists erasing Western cultures, history, and civilisation. It was the dissidents resisting that erasure.

Multiculturalists bandy about a lengthening list of our alleged phobias of other races and cultures, but it is not really a phobia to want to live according to one's culture, instead of under another culture. White people who do not fear our subsuming by other races and their cultures either do not care or welcome it: cultural genocide.

Nationalistic Multiculturalism

If we ever looked outside the West with more than a menu in mind, we would see that countries are not and never will be multicultural, as the West understands multiculturalism. Just because the West stopped believing anything worthwhile does not mean that other races stopped.

Races without racially homogenous homelands nevertheless enjoy primacy for them and their cultures in their countries. The dominant race's culture prevails, simply for being the dominant race's culture. That culture is for the dominant race to decide.

Dominant races do not defame their ancestors or cancel their cultures in deference to other races. They do not erase their religions, because some of their citizens disagree.

Feeling offence is for the dominant race. Only its feelings matter. Because they do not reward other races feeling offended, other races do not feel offended.

In a world of countries, their races and cultures dominate their countries. They permit and often mandate racial, religious, and cultural discrimination, in favour of their own.

Among the few countries with multiculturalism outside the West, it is nationalistic multiculturalism. Nationalistic multiculturalism means permitting minority races to live by their cultures, provided they do not defy the dominant cultures.

If the West truly believes all races and cultures are equal, as multicultural ideology decrees, then we need the same for our races and cultures in our countries simply for being our races and cultures. If we believe in a multicultural world, valuing our cultures as we value other cultures, we too will want cultural nationalism.

We will do what other races do. We will reclaim our cultures.

Without asking other races to celebrate our cultures, we could celebrate them. They are our heritage, with everything full lives can offer.

We fare better by asserting our cultures than denying them. We do not love other cultures by dismissing our own.

Nationalist multiculturalism would mean that we respect the rights of other races to practice their cultures, while asserting the pre-eminence in our countries of our cultures. In colonial European countries, indigenous cultures might prevail for indigenous races, but only among their own.

Other races' cultures prevail in their countries. Our and colonial Europe's indigenous cultures would prevail in our countries. What other races do with indigenous cultures in their countries is up to them.

National Identities

When asserting our cultures in our countries was not a problem, for us or for anyone else, Western countries had national and regional identities. They brought with them cultural identities, often several cultural identities. They were us and almost us, characters among us.

That so many of us were unlike our caricatures did not matter. Canadians did not need to be mounted police to feel the mounted police reflected them.

They were collectively us, if not individually us. We were inventors, scientists, artists, and engineers: some more so than others. We were pastors, soldiers, miners, and nurses. Whatever one of us did well enough, we claimed for our countries.

British and other Western cultures were not monocultures. Cosmopolitanism meant embracing the best of all Europe.

When we were not distinctive by country or region, we were distinctively Western. City people dressed much the same and wore much the same hats.

We began losing our national identities when we began losing our nations. We without nations have nothing national, no national anything, no ways of life. Worse than any lingering sense of our national identities would be a sense that anything about those identities was good.

Only the West thinks that facing outwards to the rest of the world requires us to erase our national identities. No countries face outward more than those of East Asia, but they remain emphatic about retaining their national identities.

Western countries face outwards, but not towards our peoples: the rest of the West. We face everyone else, more interested in their cultures and national identities than in ours.

Our national identities are no longer premised upon our people, cultures, and achievements. That would be racist.

Instead, they are premised upon anything else: birds, animals, trees, stars, a leaf. Our people total to nought.

We are now as likely to define our countries by cultural diversity, but cultural diversity no more defines one multicultural country than it defines another: definition without definition. Any national or cultural identity premised upon cultural diversity is premised upon other people's identities. Multiculturalism has erased our national identities.

Indigenous Cultures

Colonial European countries replicated the cultures of our motherlands, adjusted for our new settings and weather, but the people that colonial Europeans make pre-eminent in our new national identities are indigenous. They survive as identities, if without cultural traits. Anything else would be racist.

They might lack cultural traits, but their cultures survive, with the eager support that we give them. We treat indigenous cultures with great deference and humility, without critiquing them as we critique our own. Theirs are the cultures we think we should not have disturbed, however rotten they were.

The last local cultures in Europe's colonies are indigenous. They distinguish each colonial European country from the rest of the multiculturalist West.

Without anybody asking, colonial European cultures ceased to exist, as if Europe's colonies never existed. Europe is becoming the same.

Europe's indigenous culture is European, but we do not respect our indigenous cultures as we respect other indigenous cultures. Nor do immigrants.

In 2020, London mayor Sadiq Khan complained that immigrants felt no affinity with London's past. He established the Commission for Diversity in the Public Realm to replace English street and place names and landmarks, including monuments and public sculptures and other artworks such as murals, with those of immigrants.

What else did the advocates of immigration think would happen as immigrant populations grew? They never did think about it, because thinking about it would have been bigoted. It still is bigoted, even as we witness our heritage being erased.

Australia and other colonial countries had spent decades replacing British names with indigenous names. Britain was about to begin replacing British names with immigrant names.

Denied any last confidence in ourselves, we strive to undo our past cultural colonisation, while our immigrants' cultural imperialism delights us. The multiculturalist West is less of a multicultural world, because Western cultures disappear. If there is no Cornish culture in Cornwall, no Western culture in the West, they are not anywhere.

Traditions

Traditions connect us to our ancestors and thus to people with whom we share common ancestors: our ethnic group or race. Rituals and celebrations afford us structure and fun, including those commemorating lives beginning, coming of age, joining with another, and passing.

We know the right to traditions, because we accord that right to people of other races and their children. We do not demand that right for ourselves or our children.

Being individuals, we have lost our links with our forebears. We thus lost our traditions.

We have no interest in lifestyles that past generations experienced. Our only traditions are personal: those that we each make for our individual selves, one year to the next, one week to the next.

If we care about generations after ours, we will explore generations before ours, before politics and purchasing mattered so much. We will rediscover what we did before all we did was work, shop, and dine in other people's restaurants. Among the treasures our forebears can bring us, we will find again fine arts.

By reviving and maintaining our traditions, we do not just honour our ancestors. We provide cultures for our descendants.

We can honour our forebears as they sought to honour us, whatever they foolishly believed. We can care for our descendants long after we are dead, trusting them not to hate us for what we foolishly believe.

With heritages, we have futures. We would allow our rich cultural traditions a chance to survive and evolve for the better. We would rebuild and build more, without yet knowing what that will be.

Our countries might be more religious or more secular, varying over time. They have before now.

Festivals

When we were peoples possessing our cultures, the religious and irreligious possessed our religious holidays. Exuding our community traits in long-day festivals and fairs, most Western festivals involved Christianity, notably but not only Christmas and Easter. Christian festivals might have replaced our previous pagan festivals, but that is no reason to reject Christianity. It is another reason to recognise that our Christian heritage is an aspect of our European heritage.

Individualists feel no ownership of the festivals our forebears bequeathed us. Without races and nations, our only rights to religion and other culture are as individuals. They are for each of us, if we want them, in the privacy of our personal lives, away from other people's view and interaction.

We suffer no compulsion to experience our traditional festivals, but we can only want to experience them if we know what they were. We can only experience them if they endure.

When we link our culture to religion, we do not accept our religion. We reject our culture.

If just one person finds something in our culture offensive, we cancel it. Even if no person feels offended, we cancel it.

In our determination to accommodate other races, we do not risk them feeling uncomfortable about being exposed to our cultures. Our presumption that our cultures offend other races does not depend upon other races feeling offence. We just fear that they might.

Lacking as we are in all self-belief, we give up our rituals and customs that distinguished our cultures, forfeiting our festivals and fun because they were ours. We are ending our cultures, because maintaining them could seem unwelcoming of other races.

Not simply saving people of other races from being exposed to our cultures, we are also denying our children knowledge of our cultures. While schoolchildren's participation in events promoting multiculturalism is compulsory, we forbid their participation in events that are actually cultural, when the culture is ours. We dispense with Western cultures altogether.

Western public places are no places for culture, at least not ours. Preventing our people from expressing our traditions and storytelling in streets, schools, and shopping centres is not just limiting for us. It is boring for others.

Rather than presuming people of other races and religions are as absurdly hypersensitive as we have become, or encouraging them to become hypersensitive too, we might respect people of other races more by enjoying the festivals of our forefathers in our countries, as other races enjoy their forefathers' festivals in their countries and in ours. They can join us in ours, if they wish, much as we rush to join them in theirs.

Concealing our cultural heritage might disrespect them. It certainly disrespects God, our forebears, and us.

Postmodern Festivals

What remains of our culture is Christian only in name. Even that is proving too much.

Replacing Christmas decorations with something secular and supposedly respectful to other beliefs brings the West back to flowers and the like. Regressing to pagan times, we become nature worshipers.

We no longer have festivals. We have holidays, without sense that holidays abbreviated holy days: the only reason we once had not to work. With little left in Western lives but commerce, all we comprehend are workdays, weekends, and holidays.

In what the West calls progress, we regressed. Christmas becomes the nondescript Summer or Winter Holiday, with capital letters. The lack of Christ in the word 'Easter' lets that name endure a little longer, but it is becoming the Spring or Autumn Holiday.

Like our most ancient ancestors, we worship the seasons: summer, autumn (or fall), winter, and spring. If we do not imagine sharing our season worship with other races, then at least we know they will not be distressed.

The seasons we celebrate are not necessarily ours. They are

those of immigrant races, from their hemisphere of origin.

In our perfectly individualistic vision of the world, without sense of society, there are no common holidays, festivals, or anything else for people to share. Holidays are personal, for individuals to do whatever we each want to do.

Our postmodern festivals are those like coloured lights on city buildings. We can see them in our time whatever moment of night that we choose, alone in the dark or with others. They come without holidays, so people choosing not to participate can continue working, studying, or shopping.

They come without history or cultural context. The world can enjoy them without feeling that any race or religion possesses them: our best efforts towards a post-racial culture.

They also come without story, meaning, or substance. They are facile and forgettable. We are culturally empty.

Other People's Festivals

Calling Western countries secular means we separate our public lives from Christianity. It does not mean that other races separate their public lives from their religions.

While we presume that talk of Christianity disturbs people of other religions, other races displaying their religions do not disturb us. They delight us. Other religions are not as offensive as ours.

Many a religion and other culture have festivals and feast days, often fun and meaningful in the context of those cultures, with traditions a people treasure. We treasure them too, for being chances to bring everyone together, provided those festivals and feasts are not ours.

We cease Christian commemorations if just one person objects, but there is no suggestion of not commemorating other religions if someone objects. We do not submit to white people's prejudice against other cultures, although we submit to other races' prejudices against our cultures.

When people of other religions do not want Christianity confronting them, they are being sensitive, feeling justified offence. When we do not want other religions confronting us, we are being insensitive, feeling unjustified prejudice.

In our determination to welcome other races, we experience

their cultures instead of our own. When we tell other races that their cultures should be celebrated, they believe us, although they probably would have believed it anyway. When we tell them that our cultures are offensive, they believe us.

Jewish, Muslim, Hindu, and other festivals remain unchanged, as does our eagerness to wish their adherents the same greetings they wish each other. We are just as likely to wish each other those greetings, acknowledging and enjoying those religions without either one of us believing those religions. Neither people of those other religions nor we wish each other Christian greetings.

Not merely are we abandoning our cultures. We are adopting other races' cultures.

Religion by Race

"*Know Thyself*" said an inscription in the ancient Temple of Apollo at Delphi. That could be said to the West at this time in our history, such as it is.

Understanding the West requires us to know something of ancient Greece, the Roman Empire, and our religious history. We cannot hope to understand curious circles of stones like Stonehenge without knowledge of our history before Christianity.

The God of Abraham was a rare single God in ancient times, when religion reflected a natural order of things. Jews can claim the same religion they have always been, as can Africans and American Indians worshipping their ancient spirits. Hindus have a compilation of beliefs (some of them monotheistic) that might reflect ancient origins. Australian Aborigines have their Dreamtime. Other races found new religions.

Romans established colonies throughout Europe, North Africa, and the Middle East in their expanding empire, spreading civilisation. Roman religion filled Roman life, but the people who believed Jupiter was king among many gods allowed other races their sects. Each race had its religion, but the Romans persecuted the new Christian religion for purporting to be a religion for everyone, including Romans. Persecution did not deter Christians from spreading their message.

Greeks believed in Venus among many gods. They gradually became Christians.

Only in 311 and 313, when a tenth of the Roman population was Christian, did the emperors Galerius and Constantine make Christianity legal in Rome and then the Empire. Thereafter, all Roman emperors bar one would be Christian. The empire adopted religious hegemony to become the Holy Roman Empire. Her inheritor is the Roman Catholic Church.

Christian saints spread the new faith throughout Europe, while empires rose and fell. Vikings worshiping Thor and other Scandinavian gods established colonies spreading their races across the North Atlantic, before becoming Christians. The Roman Catholic Church pressed them to cease attacking fellow Christians.

A rare thing uniting Europeans was our sense of being Christian. Only Christianity among the world's religions enjoyed supranational structures, joining Europeans across nations because Rome had joined Europeans across races and ethnicities. Common Christianity was a force for peace between races.

The Eastern Orthodox Church was less centralised than the Church in Rome. Each Eastern Orthodox country had her Orthodox Church, or Churches.

With the Reformation, there arose more distinct denominations, mirroring different races and ethnicities. The Church of England was England. The Church of Scotland was Scotland. Roman Catholicism affirmed Irish, Austrian, and Polish racial, ethnic, and cultural identities distinct from their more powerful Protestant and Orthodox neighbours and foes.

We were nations united by God, if not always by religious denominations. Conflict sometimes arose between Roman Catholics and Protestants, because conflicts arise between peoples over anything they value.

While we colonised the world preaching to other races, our Christianity forged over more than a thousand years did not slip away. People's faith or lack of it mattered less than their race.

American founding father Thomas Jefferson's home, Monticello, in Virginia was a temple to European thought: a museum within a museum. His Declaration of Independence was an enthusiastic outpouring of the most idyllic ideals he had learnt from his studies in the American colonies and in Europe.

That Jefferson sought to edit the Bible to what he believed was true reflected the limits of his Christian faith. It also affirmed his Christian identity. Religious doubt, even disbelief, did not keep a

European or colonial European from being Christian.

We might not have individually been faithful, but recognised that our races were Christian. We were Christians for being Christian peoples, European, wherever we happened to live. We were Christian by birth, born to faith, even if our individual faiths faltered. Our collective Christian identity did not depend upon personal belief.

In a world with so many races not Christian, Christianity was inextricably a feature of our ethnic and racial identities, whatever our faith or without it. Western identity encompassed Christianity, with national identities no less Christian for being Christian denominations.

We identified as Christians or a Christian denomination because our people did, without dwelling upon what we individually believed. We were Christian countries and races, without us all sharing the faith.

For God and Country

Our boys who fought and died in the Great War rallied for God and Country. We did all our best deeds for God and Country, even if the people leading us to war did not.

While we have become quick to blame racial and religious loyalties for wars, such loyalties remain reasons for people of other races not to kill each other. We used to be the same.

If civilisation had a final day, it was Christmas Day, 1914. The previous evening, Christmas Eve, young German soldiers started lighting candles, illuminating their positions. Without other means of communicating, the Germans held Christmas trees above their heads, wishing the British soldiers a brave and humble Merry Christmas. They began singing carols all along the lines: "*Stille Nacht, Heilige Nacht.*"

Young British soldiers recognised the harmony. "Silent night," they sung in unison, "Holy night."

Across the tortured night on wretched ground, where a generation across Europe and her empires was bleeding to the death, the Holy Mother's love and Child made something beautiful. They were no longer soldiers killing each other and themselves, but compatriots in Christendom: a collective Christian European corpus.

They came together: sharing beer, exchanging gifts, playing soccer, and showing family photographs. This continued in some parts for two or three days as soldiers refused to resume the Great War, until their superior officers threatened them with execution. The generals, not the soldiers, resumed the war.

Far from causing war, our shared race and Christianity stopped war, in places, however briefly. Nothing else brought peace to Europe for almost four more years. Had the German and British leaderships in 1939 sensed the Christian European commonality their soldiers sensed at Christmas 1914, there would have been no World War II.

Attending church weekly had been normal before the Great War, especially among the well-to-do. After the Great War, it ceased being normal. After World War II, it slowly became unusual.

We lost confidence in Christianity not in spite of it being our religion, but because it was our religion. Science had nothing to do with it. Neither did God. Caught up with war, God ceased being a question of fact. This was no carefully reasoned analysis, but a failure of faith.

We lost Christian faith because we did not think God could allow the Great War killing to continue or to resume only two decades later, but so often when we ask how God could allow awful things to happen, we could more easily ask it of ourselves. Blaming God for our failings is much easier than blaming ourselves for what we do with our God-given choices.

We confuse causes of war with reasons our men volunteered to serve: the trusts, confidences, and loyalties. Remembering our memorials with talk of God and Country, we do not want God and Country leading us to die. We gave up Christianity and nationalism not in spite of our forebears dying for us, but because so many of them did.

War was a futile failing. Refusing for us their reasons to fight, we gave up everything we valued rather than risk coalescing around them. Slowly, we set about discarding the remnants of civilisation for which our forebears fought and died.

That is individualism. That is multiculturalism.

Without wars to fight, there can be no victories. Having lost our reasons for dying, God and Country, we lose our reasons for living.

Death

From a time that war was for heroes who came home alive, our ancestors built us countries, with farms, homes, towns, and cities. No honour or fulfilment exceeded that bearing and raising children, growing our civilisation.

So relaxed were we with death, people without photographs of their loved ones alive posed with them after they died. We loved life more than we feared death.

God in eternity made graveyards peaceful places, with Biblical and other poetic testimonials and devotions cut in stone. For the grandest graves, stonemasons carved mournful statues of cherubs, angels, and Jesus weeping. Iron palings, short enough for the living to step over them, marked some last plots of land.

That was until 1914, when death became frightening on so devastating a scale. Graves set after the Great War lie low near the ground, without saying very much: brief words on simple stone of love and loss.

So shattered by the carnage, we kicked up our heels in the 1920s, trying not to be distracted by the dead. We could not bear to think again of death.

Our lives since a second great war have increasingly become an even more reckless abandonment than they were after the first great war. We stopped considering death and valuing life. Not only wars kill men too young to die.

A century after the Great War, shades of black soil the oldest statues. Dollops of aged fungi meld into rock, providing patterns in the grey. Headstones and other slabs of stone have cracked. Iron palings have rusted.

Death remains promiscuous, but we still cannot bear to think of dying. Our graves have become innocuous, where we leave graves at all. Death hides within the names on plaques and public notices, or simply hides. People who died hide with it.

Eternity

Families, races, and religions afford people the comforts of pasts before our lives began. They afford us hopes of futures after our deaths. They afford us eternity.

For everyone who turns towards the stars or into the veins of a leaf, eternity is something more than science about time, extending without limit beyond our individual lives. It is an emotional connection to immeasurable time: a human consciousness that pauses long enough to wonder where we sit in unfathomable space and period.

It is time through generations dead and not yet born, through ancient times and peoples not so long ago. It is time before the universe began and after it ends, when the stories of our lives mean everything and nothing. At eternity, there is only God and people with Him.

Birds and animals have life and death. They do not know eternity.

Eternity can be comforting, when the past century has pained us. Without feeling our ancestral pasts as other races do, we have surrendered our sense of eternity. The end of history is the end of eternity.

Our lives are simply instants in time; that is all individuals have. Without families, races, and religion, we cannot imagine much before yesterday morning or further ahead than a week from Thursday. The world began sometime around our solitary births and will end with our solitary deaths.

Our eternity was brief. In our lives without eternity, the Great War never happened. Nothing before our births or memory ever happened.

For Western individuals without thought of time before our little lives or afterwards, eternity is just a word. Other races retain their senses of eternity, with races and religion, but only their own. They have forever for which to fight, defend, and honour.

If there is a reason above all others why individualism leaves our lives hollow, people cultureless, and civilisation tenuous, it lies in the momentariness of our existence. Our lives are predicated upon our individual selves, living so much for the moment. We cannot possess pasts or futures without feeling ourselves amidst them.

Religious Individualism

Trying to move beyond natural orders of things, collective religious identities ended in the Russian Empire with the coming of communism after the Great War. Communism separated Soviet citizens from their cultural inheritances, whatever their race and culture.

Collective religious identities ended for the free West after World War II. Not about to foist identity upon anyone, not even ourselves, we increasingly refused to identify with a group not of our choosing.

The Universal Declaration of Human Rights, which the United Nations General Assembly adopted in 1948, recognised the common correlation between collective religion and personal belief. It also distinguished them, as the West increasingly failed to do.

Religion had always been personal as well as public, but we slowly lost the public aspect of religion because we slowly lost the public aspect of everything, except economics and ideology. Thinking we could compartmentalise our Christianity and other races their religions from everything else, we stopped thinking that religion is an aspect of culture and that culture is an aspect of religion. We reduced religion to a matter of personal faith, which we each have or have not.

When we had races and nations, we had atheists and agnostics in the modern parlance, although far fewer than we have now. They did not necessarily declare their atheism or agnosticism, even to themselves.

For the most part, we in the West had long enjoyed the right to change our religion without thinking of taking that right up, much as we had long enjoyed the rest of what we came to call human rights without thinking of taking those rights up. What we came to lose through the twentieth century was the sense that religion was also our inheritance.

Religion became only something we chose, our individual decision to make, as increasingly everything became. What we choose, we can choose to refuse.

We focused upon being free to change our religion and abandon religion altogether, without appreciating the cultural heritage by which we began with a religion from birth. Western peoples without faith gave up calling themselves Christian through the late twentieth century because they gave up calling themselves by their race.

Religion and War

Through medieval times, Christian monks drained swamps, cleared forests, cultivated land, and bred cattle. Every Benedictine monastery was an agricultural college for the region in which it stood.

Monasteries conceived, incubated, and developed arts and sciences. Technological innovations included the use of waterpower and developments in metallurgy. Religious orders established schools and hospitals, developing medicine.

Early in the twenty-first century, when white people without faith think about religion (beyond our platitudes for other religions), they are not very kind. They repeat our mantra without challenge, "Look at all the wars religion causes."

Not just separating themselves from Christianity, they are freeing Islam and other religions from specific blame for warmongering and terror. They reject religion not for any argument about the existence of God but because different religions divide people from each other, from which they think all war arises.

Atheist and agnostic atrocity, they are not even contemplating. They should.

Beginning in 1789, the French Revolution rejected Christianity, demanding liberty and equality. The Reign of Terror executed more than forty thousand Frenchmen, including clergymen and women.

World War I was not a conflict between religions. The Muslim Ottoman Empire fought alongside Protestant Germany and Roman Catholic Austria–Hungary. They fought against Orthodox Russia, Roman Catholic France, and Protestant Britain. Jews were in most if not all the Christian armies.

Religion did not cause World War II. Shintoism, Buddhism, or any other religion did not motivate Japanese aggression. If Christianity was involved in the Asian war, it was Christian Americans and other European peoples defeating Japan in 1945. The atheist Soviet Union joined in at the end of the war.

A Great War veteran, a decorated war hero no less, Austrian-born Adolf Hitler became German chancellor in 1933 and dictator in 1934. Germany was Protestant, but Hitler had been raised a Roman Catholic, becoming an altar boy. Nothing in Catholicism explained Hitler's willingness to invade Roman Catholic Czechoslovakia, Poland, or France, while he made great efforts to avoid war with Protestant Britain. Roman Catholic Spain and Portugal kept out of World War II altogether.

Religion and Holocaust

Underpinning any claim that religion caused World War II is the allegation that it inspired the Jewish Holocaust, the *Shoah*. In his 1925 manifesto *Mein Kampf*, Hitler cited the Lord God to justify anti-Semitism, but he ceased being part of any church long before gaining political office. He might well have stopped identifying with Christianity, while exploiting other people's faiths.

By the time of the Holocaust, Hitler made several comments highly critical of Christianity. "The heaviest blow that ever struck humanity was the coming of Christianity," he told Martin Bormann and other close associates, among a series of informal, private conversations often late at night or early in the morning between July 1941 and June 1942, which Bormann recorded *ex tempore*. "Bolshevism is Christianity's illegitimate child. Both are inventions of the Jew."

No Christian called Christianity an invention of Jews, not then. Communism was then known as Bolshevism.

Hitler had almost certainly long been an atheist, but remains a clear example of a European we identify as being Christian quite apart from his views about God. So might he, if he was not manipulating General Gerhard Engel with a lie by telling Engel in 1941, "I am now as before a Catholic and will always remain so."

Christianity was the religion of Europe, the religion of Germans and Austrians, and so the religion of Hitler. He was born a Christian and so remained a Christian, however much he rejected Christianity and however much he might have feared being a quarter Jewish.

The perpetrators of war and the Holocaust might not have been Christian. The victims often were.

Polish nuns were among the prisoners upon whom physician Josef Mengele performed medical experiments at the Birkenau concentration camp, Auschwitz. As many as two thousand Roman Catholic clergy died in the Holocaust. They are not the victims we recall.

Atheism, agnosticism, and doubts about God so great that what remains can barely be called faith are means of Western peoples trying to separate our individual selves from our cultures and pasts, since each of the world wars and especially since the Holocaust. So is a complete ignorance and indifference towards God beyond mere atheism or agnosticism.

We have ceased to see religion as a means to salvation, just as it failed to be for Jews alighting from trains to Birkenau. The God of Moses not being real for Jews, the West came to think He cannot be real for us.

Religious Identity

For races other than ours, there is more to religion than what particular people per chance believe. Races having chosen their religions, religion remains something to which people are born. Religion is central to their races' cultural identities because they have races and thus cultures, and because religion is central to culture. Different though race and religion are, race and religion are not readily distinguished. Personal belief is something else altogether.

Religion can be a matter of identity instead of belief. The distinction can be profound.

People's religious identities reflect their racial identities. Their race determines their religion at first instance, while the West followed the communists into thinking we collectively have neither.

Race and religious identity remain wrapped together for Jews. Jews are Jews whatever their faith.

From their race came their religion. To be a Jew is to be prima facie of the Jewish faith.

Belief can be unimportant to a religious identity, as it once could be for us. Faiths lapse, identities do not. Faiths or faithlessness are there to select, but identities do not change because a person's beliefs change, or change again, because identities are grounded in unchanging races. Identity matters more than belief.

Like us, Jews might call themselves atheist or agnostic. More so than us, they might still maintain their religious ritual and identity. They might prefer to call it a cultural identity rather than a religious identity for their lack of Jewish faith, but a religious identity it remains.

Religious identities remain subordinate to racial identities, much as they once did for us. Different races and nations remain distinct, in spite of any religious commonality between them.

Muslims normally remain Muslims, even if we would call many among them atheist or agnostic for the thoughts inside their heads. Their senses of who comprises their peoples do not change because they or anyone else loses faith.

Apostasy is the renunciation of a person's religion. Islam does not normally recognise Muslims renouncing their faith; the Islamic world expands more readily than it contracts. Some Muslim countries make apostasy punishable by death, at least for Muslims. Christians in the West find apostasy almost compulsory.

The races we allow into Western countries continue the ways of their race, never too compliant with being what we want them to be or what we insist they already are. That is no less the case for the few adopting new faiths.

We no longer dwell upon what religion might mean, but whenever another race correlates with a religion, then parlance makes its identity the noun and belief merely an adjective. Hindu Indians becoming Christians are Christian Hindus, in religious terms. Being Indian remains their racial identity and thus being Hindu remains their religious identity, even if they happen to live in Birmingham and go to church.

They are betwixt and between people, but if religion were merely belief and belief was identity, then they would lose their cultural identities becoming Christians. They do not lose those identities. Losing faith, finding it, or finding it anew does not alter their religious identities, or alter the identities they see in others, including us, because race never changes.

We fail to recognise their religious identities. We fail to recognise race.

Not every race identifies with a particular religion. Most races do. Some races identify with more than one religion.

The Religion of the West

We do not condemn much, except white people and Christianity. If we are not blaming religion in general for war and holocaust, then our religion is to blame.

Rejecting any individual faith does not require people to reject their collective religion. All over the world there are young people drifting quietly away from the faiths of their forebears, without people of other races mocking their forebears' faiths as white people mock our forebears' faith.

If we returned to our past mindset and what remains the mindset of other races, we too would see that Christianity remains our Western identity. When white people loathe their heritage, they loathe Christianity. When they pour scorn on the West and all things Western, they pour scorn upon God. Separation from their race and nation becomes separation from God.

There is nothing like a chance to criticise Christians for atheists to start citing the Bible. We do not quote the Torah or Koran to criticise Jews or Muslims; that would be rude. Besides, we have no idea what is in the Torah or Koran; they are not our religion. The West only knows that they are both very reasonable.

While welcoming the religions of the rest of the world, we strive to bring our religion down. Western multiculturalism is never more virulent than when set upon Christianity.

We know Christianity to be the Western religion. That is why the faithless mock it so freely. Christianity remains our religious reference point, although white people call upon God in prayer less often than despair.

Were Christianity not our religion, particularly were we to think of it being another race's religion, then debasing it would be culturally insensitive. It would be racist.

Religious Backgrounds and Orientations

For fear of promoting religious prejudice, we stopped mentioning the religions of wrongdoers who are not Christian. We might, if pressed, speak of their religious background, which makes religion their history, although it denies them the element of choice. If people choose their religion, then it is not really background, except to the story. Religion becomes a minor descriptor, a matter of incidental fact, but a descriptor and fact nevertheless.

Those wrongdoers of other races do not diminish their religious identities as we diminish them. Suicide bombers do not go to their deaths merely as people of an Islamic background.

Similarly, we sometimes speak of a Muslim terrorist's religious orientation. It is the language we use to make homosexuality appear intrinsic to a person and so discrimination against homosexuals unjust, although Muslims continue to condemn homosexuality. We are nevertheless deeming prejudice against Muslims to be unjust, because they were born Muslim and so had no say in being Muslim.

We no longer recognise choice in homosexuality. Nor do we dwell upon the choices that other races make about religion.

If we make gods of other people, then they would probably agree, but if other races have their religious backgrounds and orientations, then we have ours. To be descended of ancient European peoples is to have a Christian background or orientation, at least for the last millennium or two, unless we think our Western capacity for choice overcomes it.

What people happen to believe can hardly change an orientation. We are still what we were in 1914, Christian European, however much we try not to be. We cannot escape our religion by birth, although the West is trying hard to reorient.

Perceptions of God affect people's thoughts and feelings about everything. So do race, family, gender, and experiences. We do not choose our race (which is much of the reason we do not like race anymore), but our ancestors choosing Christianity means we are born to the faith, just as other races are born to their faiths.

Individuals might renounce their faith and even loathe themselves for having held it, but European peoples are Christian. Ours may be the fading cloud of Christendom, but no European or distant child of Europe can speak from any other place.

Christianity and Rights

Races chose their religions, unless other races chose for them. They interpret and practice their religions as they determine, in the context of the rest of their cultures. Races can also change their minds.

Those that freely adopted religions (or bits and features of religions) did so because those religions gelled with their natures or aspirations. Different religions have different purposes for different races.

From its inception, Christianity offered people choice whether they believed in God. That came to appeal to Greeks, who had invented democracy in about 508 B.C., Before Christ. It also came to appeal to Romans and others who regarded Greece highly.

Christianity did not control people. It liberated people.

Predicated upon personal choice as other religions are not, our Christian faith shaped much of Western culture. Choices have consequences.

Unlike other races and their religions, Western Christianity never decreed rules about food and dress, although it encompassed minor disciplines by which we voluntarily experienced our faith. Our disciplines meant something to us because we followed them without compunction. We had etiquette more than regulation.

While their origins lay in ancient Greece, much of our traditional Western sense of liberties was a Christian invention. Christian Europe invented human rights, giving more rights to more people than any other race or religion has given, even if we have made a mess of them since the Second World War. We invented individuality, individualism, and their excesses. We produced the liberal democracies, even if we fail miserably to defend them.

Our traditional Western sense of rights came from our knowledge of God empowering us, but our postmodern rights do not come from God. They come from our rejection of God: our rejection of every restriction upon a person doing whatever he or she wants to do, immediately.

In the face of our relentless individualism, religion is not a matter of fact, faith, or identity. It is an imposition.

Escaping that imposition requires escaping God. Individualism becomes atheism.

We are not merely relaxed about Western Civilisation's collapse but might even welcome it, thinking we will have more scope to do whatever strange things we want to do, but we will not. Human authorities remain. Other races remain. Their religions remain.

Christianity and Science

Europe's cultural heritage encompasses much that is not explicitly Christian. The West's cultural heritage is nevertheless more

Christian than anything else: the cultures of Christendom.

The Age of Enlightenment remained an age of our long Christian era. Arguably the most important single figure in developing the Age of Enlightenment was the seventeenth-century French philosopher René Descartes. A devout Roman Catholic, Descartes believed that perfect human existence, by virtue of a questioning mind, proved the existence of a perfect God. Only something perfect could create something perfect, he reasoned.

Valuing knowledge, Christianity drew upon science, including science from times before Christ. Among the stone figures of the Chartres Cathedral are images from ancient Greece and Rome, including Pythagoras.

Artistic romanticism and scientific reason came together from the late eighteenth through the nineteenth and early twentieth centuries with our sense of God controlling a logically consistent, divine universe. Without a god or gods, there is no logical reason why the sun should rise in the east tomorrow simply because it rose there today and every day past.

Other races had knowledge, but not the laws of physics and other sciences we developed. Our faith in God's order underpinned Western science.

Our Age of Enlightenment is passed. We have multiculturalism instead.

Antagonism towards Christianity is not about science. It is about erasing Western culture.

Critics cite science supposedly to refute Christianity, without troubling themselves to learn either the science or Christianity. Nor do they cite science to refute any other religion. We do not rationally scrutinise any religions, but we irrationally criticise ours.

Christianity questioned and investigated everything. Islam proudly does not, limiting human knowledge to whatever Allah has revealed.

Our Age of Ideology is the same, but with human authorities in place of Allah. There are no sciences in our multicultural vision, as we once understood science to be. There is only ideology, without questioning or investigation.

Cultural Christianity

Second only to race, religion describes a person, as does the nihilism of atheism or laziness of agnosticism. A person's senses of deity, the universe, and human nature shape his or her every perspective.

Lives estranged from religion and religious heritage lose more than their religious culture. They leave the rest of their cultures and cultural heritage behind.

Religion is the centre of culture. It is no coincidence that the postmodern West operates without religion and has no culture, in any meaningful way. We cannot expunge our Christian culture without losing much of our Western culture.

If few white Christians feel ownership of Christian Western culture or long to experience the cultural facets of faith, then white people without interest in God or salvation are unlikely to do so, except that some do. Cultural Christians recognise their heritage better than many white Christians of faith recognise their heritage. Retaining connection to our collective religion in spite of lacking personal faith is retaining connection to our culture.

There are thus Westerners calling themselves atheist Christians, atheism being merely an adjective, much as the lack of belief we call agnosticism can be. The noun is being a Christian. They identify with Christianity.

We need not attend church to appreciate nativity scenes in shopping centre windows and Christmas carols, if not for us then for our children. Nor do we need to attend church to want to think and speak freely.

We do not need Christian faith to acknowledge the attributes that our compatriots' beliefs in a loving, consistent God bring those believers. Those qualities help others too.

According to the Book of Genesis, failing to help their poor was among the sins causing God to destroy the cities of Sodom and Gomorrah, where most sights would be immediately recognisable in many a modern metropolis. Going much further than other religions, Western Christianity taught us to help other peoples, as well as our own.

Without Christianity, we retained our enthusiasm to help others, and at least we go some way towards helping our poor. Generous is a Western thing to be, if not always with each other.

Trying to be post-Christian, the West remains Christian in what remains of our culture: a somewhat Christian Western culture, quite distinct from beliefs about God. White people hold dear our Christian European presumptions and perspectives long after their faiths have left them. Post-Christian atheists come from a different place not just to adherents of other religions but to other atheists. Western atheism is a post-Christian atheism.

If there should ever be a post-Muslim Islam, and there probably never will be, then it will be as culturally removed from the post-Christian West and post-Jewish Jewry as Islam, Christianity, and Judaism are apart and as the races practicing them are apart, however much we focus on whatever we think makes them the same. Atheistic diversity is diversity alike religious diversity. Racial diversity remains.

Christian Countries

When critics are trying to dismantle more of our Christian heritage, they complain that our countries are not yet post-Christian, as if that were an ideal that we should try to reach. When they are trying to impose another culture upon us, they will declare our countries to be already post-Christian.

If we do not reject any description of Western countries as being Christian, we describe our countries as being no less Jewish countries, Muslim countries, and countries of any other religion. Ours are supposedly countries of no religion or countries of all religions, but a country claiming contradictory religions is not a country. It is land on which different races and their religions happen to be, until a race or league of races and their religion prevails.

Accommodating other races has led to us submitting to the rules of their religions. Multiculturalism diminishes our liberties at our financial and other cost, but we will fund pretty well anything to accommodate other races.

White atheists might find that the only way they can live in the secular state in which they want to live is to live among those of their race, faithfully Christian or not. Being a Christian country is a safeguard to the faithful and faithless, and not simply for the pork, beer, and glasses of wine, or for the men and women fraternising together.

White people wanting to live in a Christian country are surely no different to people of other races wanting to live with their religions. If we are to have the same rights that other races enjoy, then it becomes beholden on our countries to be Christian, if not in faith then in cultures and laws. If our countries being Christian seem extraordinary, then notions of a Jewish nation, Hindu nation, Buddhist nations, and abundance of Muslim nations are no more extraordinary.

Outside the West, Christian nations remain. They and the Jewish nation, Hindu nation, Buddhist nations, and some Muslim nations allow people of other races to practice their religion, without submitting to their religions.

We submit. Eradicating our culture can only help other races retain their cultures. It can only help them assert theirs.

Cultural Revisionism

After World War II, many Europeans, repulsed by the preceding three decades, found socialism appealing. Englishman George Orwell's 1948 novel *1984* foreshadowed the dangers of socialism: Ingsoc being Newspeak for English Socialism.

The book introduced readers to Big Brother: the personification of a totalitarian dictatorship watching every citizen through television screen cameras, while tirelessly espousing slogans to a populace too busy to question the lies it is told. The book proved remarkably prophetic. 1984 is the year refusing to finish.

"*Who controls the past controls the future,*" wrote Orwell. "*Who controls the present controls the past.*"

Orwell could have been describing our ideological West, where cultures and histories are as malleable as everything else for political objectives. Those cultures and histories include Orwell's writing, which socialists came to claim warned us of fascism instead of socialism.

Subtler and gentler than any crudely overt dictatorship, Big Brother is more of a Big Sibling, ruling our tender West. Newspeak became normal.

Propagandists revise our traditions and cultural heritage into multiculturalism and other diversity that our forebears never imagined. Revisionism sullies our great arts to deny us our greatness. It erases our heritage.

Other races consider their cultures to be rich, but it has become inconceivable to describe any Western culture as rich, even while drawing upon it. We have been taught otherwise about our cultures, over and over, until we believed it.

Propaganda is easiest when people write, or rewrite, the stories. Revisionists rewrite our great literature, from a time in which we believed in ourselves into our time in which we do not, along its way to the screen. Revisionist stories laud the richness of other cultures while rejecting ours, ironically ours being the culture from which that literature being rewritten came. Fictitious stories can make unreality seem real and make reality seem unreal.

Historical Revisionism

The controversy over historical falsehood in fiction is an old one. Historical falsehood in what purports to be fact is relatively new.

History is a topic for a television documentary we might faithfully watch, or occasionally catch if there is nothing better to do. If a colourful documentary happens to teach us something surreptitiously, then it is not something that we need to know. Whatever we see we promptly forget, or confidently impart upon others before soon forgetting.

Relativism means there is no objective reality now and there never was. Unwilling to research pasts beyond our own, most of us have little knowledge of history beyond light film and television entertainment.

Storytellers dread telling the truth. Put another way, they espouse anti-racism themes.

True stories can be no less fictitious than fictional ones, when the objective is expunging white people's racism. The racism we condemn does not need to be real.

More telling than the omissions are the lies. Promoting racial tolerance warrants deceptions, but deceptions they are.

Amidst their revision of history, films and television programmes portray a multiracial European past that was not the reality. In October 2020, Fable Pictures announced that black actress Jodie Turner-Smith would play Queen Anne Boleyn, the second wife of King Henry VIII, in a forthcoming drama series.

We call it colour-blind casting when the colour was ours, however culturally and historically ridiculous it is. Not simply vanishing from the future, we are vanishing from the past.

Colour-blind casting only works one way: replacing Europeans with people of other races. Other races survive.

Ancient Egyptian ruler Cleopatra was Macedonian, but also in October 2020, critics nevertheless wanted the actress portraying her in a forthcoming American film to be Arab or African. Jewish actress Gal Gadot got the role.

Films and television programmes create and advance the myth that World War II defended racial diversity, instead of precipitating it because of the Holocaust. Never do our forebears' sacrifices in any war seem more futile than they seem when our soldier, sailor, and airmen forebears are erased from history, replaced by other races who never sacrificed for us as our forebears sacrificed. Never are our governments, film-makers, and others more neglectful of the people who suffered and died for us.

Owning Culture

By 2018, we were supposed to see Indian actor Dev Patel as British. When Patel played David Copperfield in the British and American film *The Personal History of David Copperfield*, not only were English people being replaced. So was our cultural heritage.

It would be one thing for Indians to make a film about David Copperfield utilising their own. It is quite another for us to make the film employing an Indian in our place. An Italian directed it.

The culture we have not abandoned, we give away. Not looking for heroes and heroines among our race, as other races like them among theirs, we throw our cultures open for everyone.

Cultural ownership is natural, sensible even, but when we of the West lost our racial and ethnic identities, we ceased possessing our culture and heritage. We ceased treating arts and learning as being those of our race. Craftsmen and women ceased being concerned in creating a culture.

We do not wonder whether anyone but Europeans could produce the memorable characters we have produced, such as David Copperfield, because we do not think in terms of Europeans producing them. Our arts and learning became those of individuals acting alone. We think only individuals produce anything.

Without collective identities, we have no architectural styles, beyond the particular homes and apartments we own. If we rent, we do not even have that.

We have no music, literature, painting, or sculpture, beyond whatever we each craft ourselves. Few of us do. We might craft for pleasure or for profit upon sale, if crafting is our profession.

Those of us unable to compose or otherwise create have no arts, beyond those that we buy. We might own canvases hanging from our drawing room walls or books on our library shelves. We might own computer discs we have not discarded or files we have not deleted. We might appreciate a painting upon which we ponder in a gallery or enjoy a song we hear from our earpieces, but never consider it ours.

Perhaps the artist feels a small sense of original enterprise, or perhaps the sale being complete her senses move along. For the rest of us, that art is not our creation. We are not a people to possess it.

With that, there is our blithe assumption that anything good one individual from our race can produce, an individual from another race can also produce. What might have been cause for our pride no longer is.

No other race produced Western science, technology, or fine arts, but when we appreciate them, it is not for being ours. They disappear into a sense of being human achievements, which all humanity possesses. We confuse the best of European nature with human nature. The whole world shares our success.

To speak proudly of our people's achievements became narrowness. Our good culture, we call everyone's culture, although our failings remain ours alone.

Cultural Appropriation

Our cultural heroes and heroines are free for other races to play: other races to become. Theirs are not.

Other races but ours do not trivialise their people's triumphs, reducing them to those of mankind. Their achievements are those of their race.

Being races, they own their cultures. With collective identities, they enjoy cultural identities. They have their pride and fervour.

They also have our pride and fervour, but we cannot have what is not ours. We must appreciate other peoples' cultures, without thinking their cultures are our cultures too. We respect other people's racial identities and so respect them owning their cultures.

When we enjoyed our racial identities, we too owned our cultures. We shared our cultures with other races without diminishing our sense the cultures were ours.

Conversely, we experienced other races' cultures, co-operating with them, without presuming their cultures were ours. Participating in each other's cultures did not require either race to submit to the other.

Today, we submit. We respect other cultures from a distance. We can only tap into other races' cultures upon the terms they allow us. Anything else, even the most innocent wearing of another race's hats, becomes cultural appropriation.

They can wear our hats. We cannot wear theirs.

Other races own not just their cultures and characters. They own what appear to be their cultures and characters, created by us.

There will be Indians and Britons who see David Copperfield as Indian, so that an Englishman portraying him would be cultural appropriation. Charles Dickens will be accused of cultural appropriation. We are not free to represent other races, not anymore.

When white people enjoy the trappings of other cultures, we complain at the cultural appropriation. When people of other races replace us in ours, we call it inclusion.

Cultural appropriation is another ideological wrong that only white people commit. We do not accuse other races of appropriating our cultures.

We fall into another ideological trap from which we cannot escape. Asserting our cultures we consider culturally insensitive to others. Adopting other cultures we consider cultural appropriation. What remains for us, except eating and drinking?

Cannot white people emulate other races owning their cultures and own our cultures too? Unable to appropriate other people's cultures should mean that we express ourselves with our cultures.

In all events, nobody needs get uppity about one race enjoying another race's culture, even incorporating it into its own. Cultural appropriation ought to be a compliment.

Haute Couture

Without racism or nationalism, when our self-appointed Western elite turn their minds to culture, it is no less estranged from their races and nations than are the rest of their thoughts and behaviours. They reserve the best of our cultural tradition to their miniature selves.

Aficionados they may be for the arts, but when they possess their cultural heritage, they do not share possession with their race. They share it with each other, if they share it with anyone. Theirs is the haute couture, European high culture: the hidden-away paintings, films, and books that few people see, watch, or read.

Without nationalism, haute couture is simply more individualism. Haute couture makers demand to craft whatever they want, without interest in sales. No worker is more embroiled in production and no consumer more self-absorbed than is the artist consuming his art that no one else does. Her self-indulgent wallowing transfixes others who self-indulgently wallow, whatever anyone else thinks.

Small audiences take great pride that the masses do not share their tastes, certain the masses cannot understand what they understand. They are right.

The fewer people who like what they like, the more elite they feel. Anything that most people see, watch, and read disappears into being commercial, thereby universal, and thereby contemptible.

Regular opera attendees believe that most people do not attend opera performances because they do not understand opera. Thus people enjoying opera do not attend opera performances because they dislike the people who do.

The most European of art forms includes ballet, but ballet teachers and schools are a world unto themselves, with no sense of a society outside or of proportion inside. Any student not willing to disfigure every bone in her body is not sufficiently dedicated. Self-absorption is never more self-destructive.

When they want to expand the boundaries of their haute couture, our cultural elites do not pursue the rest of their race:

those people they call fools who do not understand. They pursue other races, who might still not understand, but the elites are too narcissistic to notice. Artists are their favourite class, especially when those artists are coloured.

Our cultural elite save only the culture they like. So much the individuals, they save it for themselves. They are not trying to defend and develop their cultures, as other races do. They are just keeping their corners in place for a time: the time they are alive to enjoy them, or at least appear to each other to enjoy them.

What comes of their arts when they die does not matter to them, because they will die knowing that they appreciated them. They love their high culture without loving their people.

Artistic Nationalism

Our greatest arts came from artisans inspired by something greater than their individual selves. If not to God, then we in our classical periods reached above ourselves to our races and nations, drawing from strengths we sensed within us or to which we aspired. We painted, wrote, sculpted, and composed to better our cultures, as responsible as anyone to our societies and civilisation. Our arts venerated people and God.

Losing sight of our forebears, we lost sight of our artisans. We lost sight of our arts.

Having become individuals, we lack the inspiration of our forebears. We have no interest in the impact of our craft upon society, because we have no sense of society. Without race to define us, artists become defined not so much by their art as by their disinterest in anything else.

No longer glorious, our artistry now lacks optimism. Conveying no sense of our people or God, our arts do not glorify either our people or God. They might not glorify anything.

To find exaltation, we need to be more than small individuals. We need to be peoples: reclaiming and reviving our cultures, to develop as we decide.

Allowing our compatriots to participate in our personal glory allows us to participate in their personal glory. The fine arts of one of us can be the fine arts of all of us, if we find again the artistic nationalism other races enjoy.

We would create arts for the sake of our races and nations, contributing to our cultural heritage along its progression towards becoming our descendants' heritage, as other races do of theirs. The history of a race repeats in each individual.

Artistic Relativism

Our forebears knew ours to be the finest arts on earth, but they went to war and holocaust. Our rejection of our cultural heritage is our rejection of excellence.

Amidst the hubris of the time, our artists began turning away from classical styles before the Great War. Those who could not find comfort in classical art afterwards embraced ever more modernist abstractions.

We call our contemporary arts modern as if other arts were not. We call them postmodern as if anything could be.

Modernism pushed aside our European heritage. Postmodernism pushed aside everything.

Arts have become no less ideological than anything else, in this Age of Ideology. Any ideology will do.

Artistic relativism rejects the idea that any painting, book, music, or anything else is better than any other. Our postmodern arts are the arts of equality.

Our convictions of equality prevent us from judging the rubbish around us. They save us from seeing our rubbish.

What matters in our individualist West is not quality, but our individual response. That is more emotional than intellectual, as we now are.

Consumers pay attention to critical opinions, if we know what they are, because we trust human authorities. In matters of leisure, we like what the experts like, even if we quietly, guiltily see and hear what they do not, or say they do not.

For the artists, artistic relativism reduces every award to a matter of opinion. No one feels hurt, but when everyone wins, nobody wins. We do not even try.

Multicultural Arts

If we want inspiration, we no longer look to our race. We look to other races. Replacing our faces in our art are the faces of other races.

Our fine arts no longer exalt us. They exalt everyone else.

If we are not corrupting our culture, we are advocating others. Traditions in our arts we dismiss. Traditions in other races' arts we revere.

Only the West finds racial and cultural diversity exciting, because we no longer find our race and culture exciting. Racial diversity is chaotic and can boil over into conflict, but we imagine it leading to an explosion of creative energy.

In fact, creative energy does not require racial diversity. Nor does energy equate to quality. We achieved greater fine arts and other culture, sciences and sports, in our homogenous past than we have created of late.

Experts bestow their awards and rich people bestow their patronage more on politics than merit. White people succeed by supporting diversity. People of other races succeed because they are of other races.

Awards to people of other races declare those people our compatriots. They declare those races our cultural superiors.

We do not compete with other races and their cultures. We dismiss our race and culture.

There is no fusion in culture. People asserting their culture might allow their culture to be influenced. People not defending their culture let their culture abate or be subsumed.

The arts and cultures of other races develop or not according to their terms. They are in the hands of their races and nations.

Our arts and cultures are not in our hands. Our fine arts fade, before becoming something else.

The best we can hope is that mongrel arts remain with a little of our gene pools within them: some small influence our arts and cultures have upon those arts and cultures replacing ours. Most likely, they will not.

Art

"The aim of art is to represent not the outward appearance of things," said Greek philosopher Aristotle in the third century Before Christ, "but their inward significance."

Representing inward significance was not at the expense of outward appearance, in classical Europe. Our paintings were of beautiful, proud people in pretty, old places: our people and thus people.

Great paintings did not need titles because people could see what they were. The titles by which they are known today were often placed there afterwards, changing over centuries.

At our heart was Christian tradition, inspiring much of our greatest art. The Roman Catholic Church funded the Renaissance, before Christian merchant benefactors took up the cause.

There was sensitivity in classical Western art unlike other art. When wars and Holocaust made sensitivity too painful, we lost sensitivity in our art.

Religious art remains art much like other art but focused upon religion. Pursuing our postmodern vision, religious art no longer revels in religion. Religious art now rejects religion, if only ours.

Along with ideology, economics is always nearby. Art is a wonderful way for people with too much money to spend vast amounts of it; what we appreciate most about art is being rich enough to buy it. We need only to check the price tag to know whether art is quality. The more expensive art is, the better it must be.

Prizes are money for art that is too hard to sell. Nothing inflates the price of art more than experts conferring a prize on the art, or the artist.

We like art more than artists, but ours is the art that monetary artists working efficiently make: maximum output for minimal cost. Trying to earn income from art and as much income as they can, artists use lines of rapid factory production.

Art is a business much like any other, with consumers even less exacting about quality than we are with other consumption. Busy people want decorations for their offices and homes that they need not waste time to study.

Postmodern art is lazy, the work in a rush; artists making money from their profession saying they never would. Classical art's intricacies too often left artists dying poor, before their paintings became rich.

Artistic relativism means that artists in our postmodern West do not need to achieve a threshold of quality. They need only call themselves artists.

Art becomes anything that artists say that art is, exhibited on gallery walls or not. More than simply self-indulgent, art becomes transitory. We feel for a moment, leaving nothing behind.

Sculpture

Sculpture takes art from two dimensions to three. Where painting styles go, sculpting styles go too.

If our arts or sculptures portray people, they are normally ordinary, anonymous people, unless the consumer commissions a portrait or statue of himself or there is an award in the offing. Heroes and heroines have become rare in our art and sculpture, because they have become rare in the West.

Most of our art and sculpture does not portray people, at least our people identifiable as people, when we are trying to appeal to the world. Even our portraiture can be without people.

Purportedly representing every man or woman, abstract art and sculpture represent none. Geometry overwhelms humanity.

If our art or sculpture is not a job for income or ideologically explicit, then it is contemplative, for people with time to stare. Self-indulgent spectators contemplate.

Strange coloured shapes between mellow hollows do not need to mean anything. Nor do familiar objects lazily regurgitated.

Like our postmodern art, our postmodern sculptures need descriptions to explain what the sculptors say they represent. Without titles and captions, we would not know.

The figures are forms we call people, without eyes, noses, and mouths in faces once real. What remains are whatever impression each person imagines. Few of us pay much attention.

From cultural nihilism came human nihilism. Men and women vanish from our consciousness, in spite of the consumers around. Finding new ways to represent nothingness became difficult.

It is easy to see the loss of ourselves in the emptiness of our cultureless art and sculpture. When we were British or other

European, we had art and sculpture.

At best, ours are now arts without beauty: respite from the world. At worst, ours are art and sculpture without people.

Architecture and Design

Architecture is the art and sculpture of buildings. The time of great Western art and sculpture was the time of great Western architecture.

Ancient Greece provided us our senses of proportion and aesthetics, based upon human nature because ancient Greece revered human nature. In the first century B.C., the Roman architect Vitruvius associated the wide Doric columns with masculinity and the more slender Ionic columns with femininity.

Greek gods, Roman gods, and then God inspired some of the greatest architecture ever produced, forged in beauty and skill with majesty, wonder, and awe. Church architecture and design is a field of its own, with Romanesque abbeys, Gothic cathedrals, and Renaissance basilicas. Church steeples brought heaven a little closer to earth.

There was a time our buildings reached not just for the sky, but for the soul. Tall towers could be grand, when our cities were good places to live.

Styles evolved, while being Western. We saw as much beauty in what we created as in nature we did not.

Losing so much great architecture in the Second World War, we fear that we will lose it again. We only build what we need not fear losing.

Postmodern architecture follows the rules of multiculturalism. Ensuring that our architectural styles do not prevail over other races' styles, our buildings formerly teeming with culture became stylistically bland, even if colourful.

Beauty is a cost we forgo. Rarely is money wasted on motifs, colonnades, or sentiment, each of which exudes something of culture. No longer offering ornamental columns and arches, what remains is architecture without elegance.

Our postmodern churches are indistinguishable from houses, conference centres, and warehouses next door. The facilities around us are soulless. We are equally soulless.

Western buildings replaced confidence with arrogance, grandeur with ego, glory with power. We have design without décor, dedicated not to love for God or a people but to the personal aggrandisement of whatever fund or company directors approved the plans.

We are never more masculine than in the tall buildings in which we increasingly live and work, above crowded feminine shopping arcades. Our masculinity and femininity satisfied, people we do not know come to clean, watering our flower-box plants so we do not risk dirtying our factory-office fingers.

We are consumed by creating the tallest, but not the most beautiful, buildings. Simply being big is not beautiful, huge is not impressive. Unwilling to express beauty because beauty is culturally sensitive, stark and fierce are fine. So is quirky.

Engineers in urban design pursue function. Our buildings are venues for purpose.

Accountants in urban design pursue profit. In hot climes, excess glass reflects away sunlight, minimising air-conditioning costs. Reflected sunlight heats surrounding buildings, increasing their air-conditioning costs, but being self-interested individuals, neighbouring buildings do not matter.

Those neighbours are equally self-interested. Their buildings shine the heat back.

Without culture, our streets are just traffic signs, advertisements, and graffiti. At night, vandals break through wire fences sealing old buildings, spraying them with scrawls that only they understand. We have no sense of being a people owning that heritage or of the beauty they are wrecking. If Western individualism has a moniker, then it is graffiti.

Other races are not so reticent about expressing their cultures as we are about expressing ours, even in our countries. If they are not merrily building new temples and everything else in their architectural styles, they are superseding ours.

They do not care about our architectural and engineering history. They care about theirs. We too care about theirs.

We might study the architecture and artwork of old Europe, but we do not treat it as ours. Was it any cultural heritage but ours, we would all want to save it.

Homes and Houses

When we had empires, we built for empires. When we had nations, we built for eternity.

When our people mattered so much, so did the buildings we made. We built castles, cathedrals, and mansions to last forever.

When we were races, even the most ordinary of homes we built to last. Our homes and suburbs had strength, with characteristic architectural flavours.

By the twenty-first century, our heritage is not simply for sale. It is for demolition.

Our forebears could not imagine us neglecting our architectural heritage, let alone destroying it, but if we want land, we will demolish our heritage before we restore it, whenever we can. Much of our history has gone.

The elegant old homes we are trying to preserve are not our homes. They are our neighbours' homes. They are the houses short enough not to shade the sun from our gardens. They are nice houses we see through our clean lounge room windows or pass along our late afternoon strolls.

Individually minded people treat everything as individually theirs, and thus theirs to sell. We feel no sentiment for our homes, be they houses or countries. We are only at home where we feel it, and not always then. Too few of us feel it.

Like all else in our short Western lives, we individuals no longer build for eternity. We build for the moment.

Forever in the West has become the handful of years we individuals see ahead. The houses we now build need only last the short time before we sell them and go.

Without races and nations, we have nothing to endure. Our single-person homes are no less transient than our single-person lives.

Décor and Fashion

There is a reason that some styles of décor are classic and timeless. They look nice. Décor is anything that is not primarily functional.

Beauty does not cease to be beauty with the passage of time, but fashions have little, if anything, to do with beauty. Fashion demands change, driving consumers to discard the old for no other reason than being old and to purchase anew for no other reason than being new: décor without durability.

That is the case with clothes. It is the case with houses. It is the case with everything.

Culture and taste have become like everything else in the vanishing West: consumable, and buyable. When we without confidence in our culture want décor, we buy magazines or hire people to decorate. Fashion matters too much for us to trust our judgements. We might be experts in our chosen vocation, but not in what combinations of colours, patterns, and materials are fashionable and what are not. Our tastes are those that experts tell us they are.

Not to be fashionable would mean to be poor. We do not want to seem poor, especially if we are.

Commercially driven fashion decries accumulation as clutter. Spaciousness encourages more purchases. Something new is acquired. Something else is discarded. Homes become minimalist. Hoarding becomes mental illness.

Lovely lawns have become ornamental ostentation. They are not for playing or wandering. Trees are not for climbing.

The places in which we live (like those in which we work and shop) are increasingly matters of economic efficiency, not human fulfilment. We are becoming urban beasts confined to concrete boxes high in the air, standing in city pillars among streets of more pillars: shoebox apartments for which consumers pay too much money and from which we want to spend days and evenings away. They are projects for profit upon construction and sale. They are then commercial operations for lease and for living.

While we refuse to cherish our cultures, people of other races cherish theirs. Property developers design homes and apartment buildings catering to foreign buyer tastes. Foreign styles replace Western styles as foreign cultures replace Western cultures, and as foreign residents replace Western residents.

Prose

Storytelling differs between races. Western storytelling traditionally treasured the hero with flaws and the villain with virtues, drawing upon ancient Greece where even the gods had human flaws.

Christian Western storytelling retained that approach. Only Jesus was perfectly good. No other hero is.

Other races (except Jews) expect their heroes to be perfectly good. Villains are comprehensively evil.

Jewish characters are complex. Western storytelling imposes external obstacles upon characters. Jewish storytelling imposes internal obstacles upon characters: neuroses.

Amidst a Second World War, Algerian-born French novelist Albert Camus expressed in *The Stranger* or *The Outsider* (*L'Étranger*) our disconnection from our races, families, and selves. After the war, half-Jewish novelist J.D. Salinger's *The Catcher in the Rye* represented young Americans as listless and lost, without confidence in their past or elders.

The Holocaust scarred Jews and the West. It thus scarred Jewish and Western cultures.

Long before the Holocaust, Jewish psychiatrist Sigmund Freud theorised the impact that past experiences continue to have upon people. Believing Freud, Western writers came to haunt our characters with history, much as the West became haunted with the Holocaust.

Our literature once nuanced, no longer is. It is obvious.

All the races on earth want their children, and some also want other children, to read literature conveying their viewpoints. Western literature has come to abrogate all other considerations.

No longer are we teaching great literature with messages we endorse. We simply teach messages.

The messages are political. Any rubbish saying the right things will do.

We use literature for the same purpose that we use everything else: advancing our globalist vision at the expense of Western countries and cultures. No stories we like more than those of refugees overcoming the adversities they tell us they suffered, before finding happiness because the West admitted them.

They are heroes. We are saviours, but only when we welcome them.

No longer should heroes have flaws and villains have virtues in Western literature. As Nazis must have seemed to Jews at their deaths, white racists are villains for whom we countenance no virtues.

For all the fine films and books condemning white people for our supposed prejudices against others, few if any speak of other races being prejudiced against us. That would be racist.

Heroes and heroines from other races are perfectly good. Anything else would be racist.

If readers are not picking messages we already believe, we do not want messages at all. Whatever the objectives behind them, books entertain us with words without meaning, competing with other entertainment.

In the business of literature, like other fine arts, money comes from transactions: books purchased and sold. Being impatient, the first phrase of a book had better seize our attention. We might buy the book and not read beyond that phrase or first paragraph, but that does not matter. We have already bought.

Each page that absorbs us into escape encourages us onward. If the ending is happy enough, then we liked the book. We might tell others to buy it.

Without expertise, consumers have familiarity. We might read a writer, or genre, in which we enjoyed past experience. Famous writers need only their names on the cover to sell their next works; the better known the writer, the bigger the font for her name.

The success of one genre, such as magic and wizards, inspires mimicry, as does the success of any product or service, until people grow weary. Most writers have little time to experiment with anything new, any more than do readers.

Literature is a service, not a good: transient and abandoned. We no more have libraries of books in our homes than our offices. Electronic books we need not notice deleting.

The books we do not discard are decorative adornments. Never too many, but the occasional book at one end of a shelf, between shining clean bookends or beside a ceramic round vase, can make the most moronic of people seem erudite.

Poetry

The Irish especially venerated poetry and poets, the Gaelic languages being particularly rhythmic. Poetry was central to Irish cultural identity, when there was an Irish cultural identity.

Battle could seem ennobling, when the romantics thought the

world needed ennobling. *"Blood is a cleansing and sanctifying thing,"* penned Irish poet Patrick Pearse in 1913, *"there are many things more horrible than bloodshed…"*

Among the idealistic young soldiers initially setting off to the Great War was British poet Rupert Brooke. *"If I should die,"* he penned in 1914, *"think only this of me: That there's some corner of a foreign field that is for ever England."* He died in the first year of war.

In 1916, Pearse declared the Proclamation of the Irish Republic, beginning the Easter Rising. Nine days later, Britain executed him and other nationalists, spurring Irish nationalism leading ultimately to Irish independence.

A century later, if prose struggles to survive in our commercial lives, then poetry fares worse. Confined to a world in which too little beauty or romance remains and not brave enough to express ideals worth expressing, we have become the most ardent of cynics. Poetry becomes obsolete and all the poets die, before the world around them dies.

Our postmodern poets save time by writing without rhythm or rhyme. Their blank verse is industry, hurried and bland, distinguishable from business memoranda only by the matters on which they muse and because no one pays them to write. People still do not read it.

In our commercial West, ours is not to reason why. Ours is but to do and buy.

Songs

The Irish sang together in pubs. We all sang carols in the street. The best of our songs were poems with melody.

No other religion offered such melody as our Christmas carols. 'Away in a Manger' offered tenderness. 'Hark the Herald Angels Sing' offered glory.

The Psalms offered every emotion. No sound was more stirring than congregations singing: nothing more rousing than 'When I Survey the Wondrous Cross,' or more touching than 'Amazing Grace.' We heard hymns in glorious adulation of God with our peoples.

For the most part, we who stirred in years of yore to sing 'How Great Thou Art' no longer sing. We no longer stir.

Songs could have been poetry's chance to endure, but especially since the 1980s, song lyrics have become loose-fitting words, much as poetry has become. The words do not matter because we do not think about them. We are not listening to lyrics.

Bold and brassy, we hear noise without music, poetry without rhyme and rhyme without poetry. They are barely discernible words we cannot decipher.

Rhyme alone does not make music good. Rap music rhymes.

No wonder the songs became louder: emotion without meaning. Feelings without relationship are individualism.

Without us asserting our culture, the songs around us no longer resound with Christian faith. They scream hostility towards it.

Our postmodern church music became like the rest of our monotonous music. Songs might speak to our devotion, but they are about each individual us, not about God or Christendom: a congregation in which we stand.

We repeat banal lines over and over, because we repeat everything over and over. Repetition saves writers from needing more imagination. It saves singers from paying attention.

Music

The definitive classical composer Ludwig van Beethoven was German, but we are doggedly determined not to own anything good. Sometimes bandied about is the nonsensical claim that Beethoven was black.

If we really believed Beethoven was black, we might again listen to his orchestral melodies. Young Germans might appreciate his Pastoral Symphony. We do not listen to our musical heritage, because it is ours.

Like the rest of our arts, God and Europe inspired our classical composers. Gone are the background violinists and other subliminal soft musicians. Patrons listened. Matrons conversed.

No longer basking in Bach, music has become about multiculturalism. The West never sets our nets wider than when we are in the mood for music.

Repetitive thumping thuds evoke African drums. Aggression is the emotion we want.

Loud modern music saves us from conversation, leaving us

comfortably compliant and alone. Thinking is intellect, but no one can think. Talking is relationship, but no one can talk. The solitary fool fares no worse than the wise with family and friends.

Radio stations play music energising us to compete. Supermarket and other store sounds push us through our most immediate commercial activity. Heavy, pulsating beats like racing hearts pump us towards our next purchases like addicts hungry for drugs.

If melodious music and soulful song have their place, it is commercially chosen. We do not appreciate music as much as we appreciate electronic sound systems.

A symphony is not a symphony without someone to play it. In spite of recordings of great symphonies performed by the finest of orchestras, a symphony is not a symphony without someone to hear.

Dance

We used to waltz, to promenade. Men worked and women beautified ballrooms with European grace, dwelling upon each other's eyes. If not courtship, dance was companionship.

Dancing the twist in the 1950s and '60s, men and women no longer dwelt upon each other's faces. At least we still held each other's hands.

Dancing, men and women no longer touch. Barely are we able to recognise each other through the crowd, whether in darkness or light. Friends, lovers, and strangers become indistinguishable on the floor of a dance. We dance like we live, but to music.

Our dance is no less African than our music. We have become chaotic, bouncing around in dark crowded nightclubs or beneath garish coloured lights at less-crowded company events.

Seldom have we still courtship or companionship. We have become individuals.

Celebrity

Our favourite entertainers used to be the most talented or engaging. They enjoyed the best tutors and mentors.

They have become those we are most accustomed to seeing or hearing, salaciously or otherwise. They enjoy the best publicists and marketers.

We do not need arts anymore. We have celebrities.

Among the many careers available to aspiring consumers in our vacuous, image-conscious West, one career is simply being famous. The celebrity is famous for no other reason: the marketing of self over substance, a person purely as image. A celebrity's talent for doing anything matters less than a publicist's talent for promotion.

Notoriety need not be privacy's loss. An image with stories to tell can be confined to the peripheries of a performer's life, or be contrived altogether. The most publicised name around does not need to confess anything about the person behind the name. It is probably better if it does not.

The person might be too weird. The person might be too normal.

Performers' personal lives were once more reason to like them, particularly when they married and became parents. They have become more entertainment, particularly when their lives are spiralling downwards.

Intrinsically individualistic egos can be brittle great beasts, depending upon fame and the adoration of strangers. Photographers and journalists torment troubled stars because, somewhere beyond magazine editors and television programmers, voyeurs pay money to watch. Entertainment is news and news entertainment.

Theatre

Englishman William Shakespeare remains widely recognised, not just in the West, for being the world's greatest playwright. He was not our only great literary figure.

Our Western inheritance accorded us a lifetime of great story, theatre, and oratory. The only languages worth learning were our own, including our Latin heritage.

That was until the Holocaust. British playwright John Osborne's *The Entertainer* expressed the empty Pyrrhic victory of World War II, finding comfort afterwards not in our race but in other races. Without faith in ourselves, we found consolation in races over which we previously felt superior.

Plays portraying the decline of the American South were the decline of white America. They were the decline of the West.

Escaping our decline and competing with cinema, theatre became increasingly musical with spectacular special effects. It became less profound, less painful.

We now keep from the stage anything denying our self-disbelief or challenging the greatness of everyone else. We prefer to let people of other races perform our great plays, or we corrupt our plays into something not great.

Other races like seeing their race on the stage. We like seeing other races, too.

Filling our homes and schools with works and images of Shakespeare and others could inspire our children with our heritage, but we cannot inspire them with what they do not know. Amidst our globalist multiculturalism, Western cultural figures fade. Without us teaching our children our artistic doyens, and indeed our heroes and heroines, our children will not learn of them.

Races have their tales, while we also produced fairies. We could seem so playful and whimsical, but by the twenty-first century, we wanted to hide.

Films

Probably the most accessible reminders of what we once were, with hints of what we could have become, are old films. If they seem to have dwelt too much on the best we could be, it was because we wanted to be the best we could be. All our arts sought to build us, even while drawing our attention to failings we should remedy.

World War II jarred us into a deeper nihilism than had the Great War, ushering in the foreboding film noir. The West all became a bit German. Blonde-haired women were *femmes fatales* because Nazi Germany so seductive proved so destructive.

We relaxed our cinematic codes in deference to Jews, telling their stories of Holocaust. No longer were film-makers catering to Western sensitivities. They were trying to change Western sensitivities.

Overarching it all are political objectives. Our films became no less ideological than the rest of our arts and the rest of our lives.

Nothing is more important than eradicating white racism. Characters from other races became kinder and better than we are. Rarely are they villains or threats.

Aliens once threatening became benevolent, while warmongering humans need lectures in peace. Our enemies became Western authorities, as they were to Jews through the Holocaust. Viewers identify with the oppressed.

The sympathies we feel for other life forms in films, we came to feel for other races in life. We should not be any less sympathetic towards them if they are not always peaceful. We are not always peaceful.

Our forebears, parents, and God used to teach us about life. Films now teach us to learn about life from wise other races and beings. Hearing of bad deeds by other races became unsettling.

Like so much of our arts, screenwriting became lazy, contriving conflict with cursing and cussing rather than character and predicaments. For all the swearing some people make, no person can rival second-rate characters in third-rate film scripts, or even otherwise first-rate characters in otherwise first-rate scripts.

More blatantly than the rest of the arts, films are not trying to advance Western Civilisation, but to degrade it. Everything about films is more blatant than other fine arts.

Films no longer glorify us. They terrify us. The best we can do is find new ways to shock.

Our most prevalent film villains became zombies: the dead. With nothing to fear from other races, our compatriots who die in the first act of the story try to kill us in the second. They are our past: our ancestors and parents. We can believe they would be hostile to us, thinking they were hostile to other races. No guardian angels from seats beside God, they are monsters from hell's deep ravines. They are us, when we die.

The Solace of Television

Secure in our homes, we prefer watching television to attending the cinema for the privacy, and for the ease of looking away when our concentration stalls. Television is cinema with an exit strategy.

Not content with complaining there is nothing to watch on free television, we subscribe to pay television and computer streaming services. We still complain there is nothing to watch, save for the sport, but watch anyway.

We watch new versions of old programmes we do not realise we have seen and watch old programmes because they were better, by subscription or hired for viewing at home. We do not keep libraries of films and television series any more than we keep libraries of books. Discs bought are easily discarded.

We can comfortably experience a programme or film without effort, relying upon other people's imagination without imagination of our own. Some of the best writing of late, and the most influential, has been for watching at home. Anything coming through our computer or television set had better carry us away within the first few minutes or we will abandon it, although we might leave the computer or television set playing while we watch a smaller computer screen in our hands, or move around our abode.

The screens bring sound and movement: noise and presence giving each solitary person some semblance of company, activity around us. They are background that nobody needs notice, not forcing us to think. Canned laughter alerts audiences to jokes that we would otherwise not notice.

Like other consumption, television can be human experience, without the intrusion of real human beings. In fairyland can be relationships, lingering the joys and terror, pains and love, we do not feel in the rest of our lives. Preferring happy lies to miserable facts or crying for characters unreal, we want comfort and consolation when actuality hurts. In fantasy are none of the complications that reality can be.

We do not readily delineate actors and actress' performances from the rest of their lives. Sometimes, neither do they.

Our best friends are fictional characters in series and serials for their repetition, returning each day or week that we are not otherwise engaged. They are artificial friends, pretend-people in pixels like those in print, but without anything peculiar to individual imaginations. Their hopes and fears, likes and dislikes we know better than we know our own, or anyone real.

Sprightly talking and laughing, they demand nothing of us, while our thoughts are with the meeting at eight o'clock in the morning or the black cast-iron table advertised in the last commercial break. Without angst upon anyone, our times together end when we press the buttons on our remote control handset or wipe our fingers over the screen.

Television Themes

Much of what happens with films happens with television, but week after week, day after day, night after night. Ours are the generations shaped by television.

In the 1960s, witches, weirdoes, and aliens were often friendly family people. They could be funny, too. Our vision post Holocaust moved from merely tolerating diversity to trusting it.

Meanwhile, racist film or television characters were working-class buffoons, at whom audiences laughed. Increasingly they became more middle class and loathsome. They were always white.

By the 1980s, rich characters did not need to be racist to be appalling. They were unrelentingly awful in spite, or perhaps because, of their good looks, fine clothes, and big mansions. The richer and more beautiful they were, the worse they were, much like the West seemed to Jews.

We mock our old books and films for their racial stereotypes grounded in the reality of their eras. We accept new racial stereotypes at odds with reality in ours.

Children's television became the most obvious forum of fantasy, with white criminals and idiots, coloured police and genii, and interracial relationships and adoption so normal as not to be noticed. We are determined to avoid reinforcing negative stereotypes about other races, however truthful they are. The safest course is to create positive stereotypes about other races, however untrue they are.

We welcome negative stereotypes about us, however untrue they are. No longer are we supposed to assume nothing about the races of criminals. In spite of our experiences and those of people we know, as well as the reality of the world at large, we are supposed to presume criminals are white before imagining they could be anything else.

Trusting Western popular culture, we need only fear white people. If film and television villains are foreigners, they are more often than not the same foreigners they have been since the Second World War: Germans, Russians, or Serbs, but always white.

The Broken West

Increasingly since the Great War, and especially since World War II, we have been lied to, as no other race in history has been lied to. We are still being lied to, as no other race on earth is.

We also lie to each other. Some people feel compelled to lie by their circumstances. Others speak untruths, unwilling or feeling unable to consider whether their words are untrue.

They are lies and untruths about history and about different races today. They are lies and untruths about human biology and nature. They are lies and untruths about us: that we are a race or races; that we have cultures or that anything about our cultures is worthwhile; that we ever were a civilisation.

"*The Party told you to reject the evidence of your eyes and ears,*" wrote George Orwell. "*It was their final, most essential command.*"

Orwell's words could be applied to everything we are told about race and gender, early in the twenty-first century. Wanting to know the truth has become wrong, when the truth is anything good about our race or not good about another race or about different races living together.

Complaints of privilege, supremacy, cultural appropriation, institutional or other racism, and other demands of multiculturalism are thinly veiled enmities against white people. They empower other races to tell us what we must do and not do, amidst the normal racial conflicts that we refuse to acknowledge.

Other races assert themselves, because we let them. We submit to our decline, celebrating every advance by other races and replacement of ours, crushed by everything pressed increasingly down upon us since 1945, 1939, and 1914. We cannot so much as stand up for ourselves.

Rather than resist people maligning or harming our race, we yield to them. Convinced that defending ourselves, our forebears, or our descendants is wrong, we are a broken race. We are broken races.

We have been broken by propaganda, immigration, and all the structures of our countries turned against us. Worst of all, we have been broken by our race turned against us.

Saving the West

Other races are not as submissive as we are. Races retaining their self-confidence assert their accomplishments, as we do not assert our accomplishments.

At our best, we became trivial Europe, consumed by a sense of equality. So certain are we that all races are equal, it follows that all races achieved equally: artistically, intellectually, technologically, and so forth.

All races did not achieve equally. They did not even come close to achieving equally. They still do not.

Standardised time is now normal the world over, but British railways invented standard time, Greenwich Mean Time, in 1847. New Zealand was the first country to introduce standard time nationwide in 1868.

If we were as fair minded as we insist that we are, then we would appreciate that European races do most things very well. We would judge ourselves not by our most terrible years of twentieth-century war, but by the totality of all we have done and tried valiantly to do. Thousands of years of history before 1914, and many a moment since then, testify to how great a race and races Europeans can be, in Europe and elsewhere.

Telling the truth of Western history, cultures, and civilisation might inspire immigrants to join us in forging new common identities, supplementing our racial and religious identities. The truth could overcome, in part, some of the divisions inherent in multiculturalism.

That would depend upon us wanting the truth. We would need to be willing not just to believe in ourselves and our forebears, but to defend ourselves and our forebears.

In spite of all we have been told and all we so assuredly believe, the reality remains that a world without white people, or without white people in meaningful numbers, would be less able and willing to feed, clothe, and house people: to deal with challenges and threats of any kind. It would accomplish fewer fine arts and other arts, however uninspiring much of what we have produced of late is. It would achieve less in the sciences. It would produce fewer ideas and philosophies, although we have produced few of those worthwhile of late. Most importantly of all, a world without white people would be less beautiful.

Modern-era missionaries will not save the West by knocking on doors of people reading books or watching computer screens alone, but might save the West by producing what people read, see, and hear. Well-written stories, well-performed songs, and well-made films by people skilled in persuasion ought to fare better than anything mediocre to convince people the truth of the truth, even if that does not seem so through this ideological period.

Censorship

We need to be careful. We need to be subtle.

For anyone saving the West, the only literature now worth writing offends a white populace convinced that the West should not be saved. It offends other races knowing how incredibly sensitive we are to their feelings: how much we reward them for feeling offended, or for saying they feel offended.

It is nigh on impossible for writers to be heard if publishers disagree with their words. Publishers do not care what people happen to think if those people are not buying books. They do not always care if they are.

Censors once banned books and artwork for being dishonest or immoral, undermining civilisation. Some people burned them.

In this Age of Ideology, words, pictures, and people are set upon for being truthful or moral, defending civilisation. Thus the people who once opposed authorities banning books would now ban books themselves, all be they different books.

People eager to ban books prove equally eager to burn them. They might not burn people, but they threaten to do so.

They remove paintings and monuments for much the same reason. They pull down and destroy statues, but only of us.

The West having become convinced that our forebears shared our views of the world, we are appalled when an old record reveals a person thinking otherwise. Unable to see that person's attitude as normal for his or her time (and still normal for the rest of the world) and whatever his or her achievements, we dismiss that person as we dismiss dissidents today.

He or she becomes another person whose work and arts are prohibited. His or hers is another name to strip from streets and from buildings, another statue to tear down. All record of him or her vanishes.

The Future

Like other media, wide-release films and television programmes reflect some of the values we hold, while promoting the values we will hold. If films and television do not prophesy the future, they dictate it.

From 1966, the American science fiction television series *Star Trek* still offers our most optimistic vision of the future. It describes a universe in which different races and species work safely and mate together without vanishing. Without religion or other culture aside from eating and drinking, and without money, it is communism at its most fanciful, but with American colour and flash.

Since then, the future portrayed in film has for the most part become darker, more cluttered, and bleaker, much as it did in Germany after the Great War. It has become increasingly post-national and even post-racial, with everyone individuals on individual quests, but only in the West.

Sometime, it all became soulless. Our fine arts and rest of our cultures reflect the post-Holocaust West's deep nihilism and fatalism.

Death is inevitable and life outside our control, we feel, however good or bad we are. At any moment, we could die, as so many of us died through two world wars and so many Jews died through the Holocaust. Many more of us could have died through the Cold War threatening us thereafter and through every danger since then.

There is no morality or sanction in the shadows of our demise. No less than the power we feel over all the races on earth, and even the Earth itself, is the sword of Damocles hanging above us.

Depraved, debauched, and doomed, dark days for Europe are dark days for the world. The West that films and television portray is often worse than reality, but reality is trying to catch up. It inspires the broken West to accept our decline that we think we can do no more than massage.

We lack the racial unity to redress our decline. We lost the self-belief to want to.

There are moments of exception. Black Lieutenant Uhura recognised Christianity, if only her knowledge of it, at the end of a *Star Trek* episode in 1968, visiting a futuristic planet where the Roman Empire never fell. "Caesar and Christ," reflected Captain Kirk. "They had them both, and the Word is spreading only now."

Well might we speculate what the British Empire might have become without the Great War. We could have enjoyed growing knowledge and technologies, with civilisation.

Were we to recognise the devastation that the Great War wreaked upon us, then we would recognise World War II and the Holocaust as consequences of that devastation, with devastation and consequences of their own. We could start to live around them, dealing with those consequences: multiculturalism and diversity.

We could resume being what we would have remained, but for the Great War. We could again be Western: Christian ladies and gentlemen, revering our pre-Christian past, most obviously ancient Greece and Rome. We could again be human: natural, tribal, territorial, surviving. Most profoundly of all, we could strive for our future as other races strive for theirs.

The West will not survive, unless we want to survive. Our race will not survive, unless we want to survive. That means treating our race and cultures as people of other races treat their races and cultureless: being unapologetically racist and nationalist as they are.

2. CHRISTENDOM LOST

The most remarkable feature of people in places of worship is not how different they are from people outside, but how similar. Whatever the race and religion, race more than religion defines and describes people, however much we of European heritage disregard both. Religions are distinctions within races.

The same titular religion differs between races because races differ. European Christians are as different to African Christians as Europeans are different to Africans, and so forth.

Early in the twenty-first century, we have much to learn from other races about identity, loyalty, and conviction, whatever their religion. They believe what they used to believe, or do not dwell upon what they do not believe. Whether they learn anything from us, is up to them.

Other races remain races, retaining their religions because they retain their cultures. Their churches and other religious authorities defend them.

Not us. The Church that once defended Christendom no longer cares.

Without Christianity or other nationalism to ground it, Western Christianity fractures along the same fault lines as does everything else Western. We of the faith are no less responsible than anyone else for the decline of Western Christianity and the rest of Western Civilisation. We of the faith offer people no more reason to be Christian than does the rest of the vanishing West.

Western Christianity

We used to be Christian for being European. Being Western still determines our religion.

Western peoples of faith are much like those without faith. We always were. We changed together.

Traditionally, we understood Biblical teaching by study and

reason. Christianity commands the truth, but when the West lost interest in facts, so did Western Christianity. We ceased studying or reasoning.

Our churches no longer lead the West, if they ever did. They follow. Western churches are more Western than churches.

We do not rationally interpret the Bible and preach God's Word to the world. Instead, we accept every dictate of the ideological West and preach the West's word to God.

No longer trusting God and the Bible, Western Christians trust human authorities and their decrees of what is right and wrong. Sin ceases to be disobedience to God, but becomes disobedience to those authorities. With the success of human authorities in determining public opinion, sin becomes disobedience to public opinion.

We interpret the Bible accordingly, affirming what we want the Bible to mean. We redefine Christianity to be less in God's image and more in ours. We call our resulting religion Christian because we are Western, but ours is Western Christianity.

God has not revised the Bible. We revised it, to what we want it to say. We preach the word of man, not God.

Having lost interest in what Christ had to say, we presume Christian obligations that are not in the Bible, but are our postmodern impression of what goodness should be. There is no Biblical multiculturalism, individualism, or diversity, no general Biblical command for inclusion. The Bible only mentions tolerance to condemn tolerance of wrongdoing.

Biblical truth is something else altogether. Western multiculturalism depends not just upon us trusting other religions. It depends upon us not trusting ours. Western Christianity is eroding from within.

White Christians are no more interested in Biblical teaching with which they disagree than are white people without faith. Western Christianity has become as ideological as everything else Western, in this Age of Ideology. Just another expression of ideology, Christianity becomes pointless.

Christian Individualism

The only races to have taken up individualism since World War II were not just Western. We were Christian. We ceased being Christian peoples not because we ceased being Christian, but because we ceased being peoples.

Dispensing with religious loyalties after the Jewish Holocaust, Western churches and church schools were at the forefront of turning our racial loyalties upside down. While we support and advance other races and their religions, there became no turning the other cheek to white people's racism.

Neither the faithful nor faithless still think of us being Christendom, a collective Christian corpus, as we did until 1914, did to some degree until 1939, and even to some degree through to the 1960s perhaps. We are no longer Christian for being of the Christian West. We are simply Christian or not.

Everything white people do to talk down white people and talk up other races in pursuit of inclusion with other races, white Christians do to talk down Christianity and talk up other religions in pursuit of inclusion with other religions. The result is the same degrading of our religion as of our race.

We have succumbed to a Christian individualism. Single-person faith means our faith is no reason to identify with others, not even others sharing our faith. Our Christianity no longer connects us to other Christians, any more than our race connects us to others of our race. We are estranged from each other when we stand before God, and in the rest of our solitary lives.

We reject priority for Christianity in our countries because we reject priority for our cultures, even if we have personally kept the faith. It was all very well for the Holy Father, Pope Benedict XVI, to want Europeans to rediscover our Christian heritage, but Western peoples of faith are no more embracing of our European heritage.

The Apostle Paul said the Galatians could keep their cultures. Cannot the rest of the West?

Without countries and cultures, Christians are no less fixated than other white people with commercial expansion. Where our companies go, our churches go too.

Throughout the West, our churches are becoming cafeterias, antique stores, and magic shops, if not mosques. Christianity dwindles and withers in Christendom, but losing our churches matters to us no more than losing our countries. The decline of Western Christianity is symptomatic of the end of our collective identities: our races and nations. The dissolution of our churches mirrors the dissolution of our countries.

Belonging

At the core of our civilisation the West now rejects were not merely the cultures in which we lost confidence, the rules we came to resent, the mores and morality we came to malign, or even the salvation we desperately need. It was the belonging we individuals crave.

Religion offers a sense of belonging to a moral community based upon religious faith, centred upon intimate circles of friends who share a similar identity. Community requires tribalism.

The West rejected religion when we rejected belonging: racism and nationalism. Western peoples ceased attending church not for ceasing to be Christian, but for ceasing to be peoples.

Even those keeping the faith have lost our broader belonging. We identify with Christianity, even consume bits of it, but we are individually Christian, not citizens of a country or race. We might have company in church, but only for as long as we are there. Each of us sits alone. Away from services, church doors are locked.

Without collective corpora, we individuals have no families, races, or nations. We have no churches. We have no belonging.

Having lost interest in our peoples, we are preoccupied with our private little faiths. We pursue our perceived personal salvation, dwelling upon our inward senses of God without reference to religion. We do what we want to do, certain that it is what God wants us to do because we want steadfastly to do it. We settle upon our single-person beliefs without regard for their effects upon the rest of our race. Our compatriots do the same.

We have our faith. That is enough. Our faith, fulfilment, and security mean everything, but only to us.

To everyone else, our faith, fulfilment, and security mean nothing. The best thing is never to mention them.

Social Justice

We are no less divided by class inside our churches than outside.

Championing others more than our own we call social justice, but they are other people's societies. We are individuals, with no more thought of our race than those without faith: the injustice of neglecting our own. Why would people sit in churches more interested in everyone else than in them?

Instead of society and justice, we have social justice. The West's ideological social justice is premised upon us having no societies and our disinterest in justice for white people.

We help everyone, but when there is a conflict between Western interests and other races' aspirations, as there constantly is, we now favour other races. We do not side with Christians. We do not side with our race.

Our only difference with white people without Christian faith is our presumption that we act with God's will. It is as if God too prefers other races and their religions to us and ours.

Aside old-style Christendom, our private individual religions are rather small. We have little engagement with people, except on our terms; the choices that matter are ours. If we evangelise, then it is because we feel called to evangelise. We do not care if we succeed, so long as we try.

Headed to heaven without regard for the faith left on earth or the world after our far-coming deaths, our interests are in our afterlives, not anyone else's afterlife. We are self-contained Christians, not trying to retain or restore Christendom or Christian countries. Religion has no link with our nation or society, because we have no nations or societies with which religion can link. For the sake of our small visions of ourselves, we walk away, while our compatriots can all go to hell.

Asylum Seekers

Western churches make much of Christ's command to welcome a stranger, but it is among a litany of commands to help people in need. The stranger is not simply someone seeking a better life.

The stranger is among Christ's brethren. The stranger is Christian.

Christ never says we should surrender our home to a stranger. After granting our hospitality, even shelter for the night, we should bid strangers on their way.

Western churches claim that the Holy Family was like today's asylum seekers. Commoditising Joseph, Mary, and Jesus with thugs, vandals, and liars without interest in Christianity or in us, even hostility towards Christianity and us, is an affront to God.

Joseph and Mary were not refugees in Bethlehem. They went there to register for a census ordered by Caesar Augustus. Not getting a room for the night does not make someone a refugee.

Equating Joseph, Mary, and Jesus fleeing the Massacre of the Innocents with today's asylum seekers equates fleeing the murders of babies with headed somewhere wanting money. Asylum seekers today are not fleeing their pending deaths.

After the Massacre of the Innocents passed, the Holy Family returned home to Nazareth. Today's asylum seekers return home on holidays (as the Holy Family did not), but few go back to live.

Christians outside the West do not demand their countries welcome immigrants. Justice and mercy for their forebears, compatriots, and descendants demand that they keep outsiders at bay.

When Western churches speak loudest, we no longer speak for our race. Our churches would rather give sanctuary to illegal immigrants of other religions than keep sanctuary to white people of our religion. We are denying our race not special sanctuary, but any sanctuary.

We welcome the world, come what may. Immigration is against the future of Western Christianity, but Western churches are unwilling to save themselves any more than they are willing to save the West.

Christ does not say that we should let our people suffer, but we are willing to let white people suffer and die to provide people of other races better lives. In effect, we are killing each other, claiming to be kind.

We are Christians without countries. A suicidal Church is taking the suicidal West with it.

Biblical Races

The Bible is not always a book to read precisely, like a recipe book. In ancient times, information was not conveyed in such terms.

It is a literary work. The poet might not mean every phrase to be technically true, simply because it is true.

Other times, Biblical passages are precisely true, with logical applications and extensions for other times and places, including ours. Distinguishing the two can be difficult.

The distinction is often unimportant. God creating the universe matters more than whether He took seven days doing so.

Adam and Eve might have been metaphorical. They might have been the first of our race, or the first of their race. All people might not be related.

White Christians dwell upon men and women being made in the image of God (whatever that means) as a reason to embrace every person on earth. Doing so disregards everything else in the Bible.

In the Bible, relationships are biological. Being raised by Egyptians did not make Moses less of an Israelite. Family and tribe are matters of blood.

Both Testaments speak to races and nations. If people think the Apostle Paul declares race not to be real when he says there is neither Jew nor Gentile but one in Christ Jesus then they must also think that Paul declares gender not to be real in that passage. No more denying one than the other, race and gender remain.

Paul simply told the Galatians that they could retain their Celtic and other European culture without adopting Jewish ritual. Similarly, Jews becoming Christians could keep their Jewish culture. All European peoples becoming Christians could keep their cultures. Other races becoming Christian can keep their cultures.

The Bible does not shy away from generalisations with racial connotations, although identifying the race along with the geography can be problematic. In our postmodern parlance, Paul is a bigot for his comment about Cretans. The Bible being divinely inspired, God is also a bigot.

The Bible and loving God remain racist and nationalistic without diminishing the opportunity Christ brought all nations and races to follow Him. Some nations and races do. Others do not. We used to.

There are as likely to be races in heaven as there are to be genders, families, tribes, and nations. There is as likely to be racism as there is to be familial loyalty, connectedness, or relationship.

Biblical Nations

The Bible speaks of believers and God fearers. Nations encompass the faithful and faithless. Personal faith or faithlessness need not divide families, tribes, or races.

God commands tribes, clans, and families to retain ultimate control and title to their territories, even if they lease them to others. Among the many interpretations of the Tower of Babel and of the Whore of Babylon is condemnation of international superstates: globalism.

Undeterred by the Bible, Christian individualists do not believe in countries in any meaningfully defined way, not for the West, although we respect countries for other races. National borders, sovereignty, and body corpora are as real as we want them to be, but if they are unreal for countries, then they are unreal for people. If national borders and sovereignty are not real, then private property is not real, but the books of the Bible defend peoples' territories.

Our globalist West encompasses everyone equally. The Bible does not, expressing words and sentiments our vanishing West would call xenophobic and racial vilification.

The Bible talks of foreigners, thereby affirming races and nations. At a time that other religions imposed no obligations to outsiders, the Bible spoke of them, with limits. We have lost those limits.

People living by Scripture do not risk harming their compatriots, but may let foreigners use what we cannot use. Kindness to foreigners is not at a people's expense. A punishment for abandoning God is serving foreigners, giving up our countries.

Love thy neighbour is a command of kindness to our compatriots, including those we do not know. It is the sense of community underpinning racism, nationalism, and other tribalism. In certain instances at least, Israelites excluded foreigners and people of foreign descent.

Globalism will fail. The Book of Revelations foretells a world worshipful of God comprising tribes and nations.

Jewish Guilt

Biblical guilt and innocence are not just for individuals but for whole families, tribes, cities, and nations, with the opportunities and responsibilities that entails. Goodness and favour spare not just the innocents but their families too, while whole peoples are punished and rewarded. God's justice can be racial, without diminishing His love.

The people we now call Jews might well have been among God's people of the Old Testament, but they rejected His Son in the New. Jewish authorities were complicit in the Massacre of the Innocents by the brutal part-Arab Jewish King Herod trying to kill baby Jesus.

It is easy for Jews to treat Christians as being wrong. They dismiss the New Testament, essentially keeping what we call the Old Testament, and await the Jew who will be the messiah.

In Christian eyes, Jewish racial guilt for Christ's Crucifixion flowed from Roman governor Pontius Pilate telling the Jewish crowd that Christ's death was the crowd's responsibility. The Jewish crowd replied: "His blood is on us and on our children!"

Biblical or other analysis did not end Jewish collective guilt for Christ's Crucifixion. The Holocaust did, although Nazi dictator Adolf Hitler would not have cared who killed Christ. Jewish guilt for Christ's Crucifixion rarely, if ever, inspired anyone to harm Jews.

Any Biblical foundation of anti-Semitism does not lead us to be anti-Semitic. It leads us to be anti-Biblical.

Anti-Semitism matters to the West. The Bible no longer does. In 1965, a Vatican II document, *Nostra Aetate*, declared that we could not attribute Jesus' death to all Jews.

In our postmodern, relativist frame of mind, historical and other facts are no more important to Western Christianity than they are to anything else in the West. Western Christianity declined after the Great War, but began dissolving altogether in response to the Holocaust.

Western Guilt

God chose Europeans to spread His word from Christ's birth, if not before. He might have chosen other races too.

Saint Peter and others brought the chance to be Christian to Rome, which brought the chance to be Christian to the rest of Europe. Europeans took the chance to be Christian to the rest of the world. Most of the world did not take it.

Since the Holocaust, the West ceased thinking that peoples chose God or that God chose peoples. There are no God's chosen people, least of all us. We are not chosen by anyone.

Nor are we people who once chose God. We are not a people at all, but a motley array of individuals.

That is, except in matters of guilt. There, our aversion to race drops away.

The end of Jewish collective guilt ushered in the West's collective guilt. Our racial and religious culpabilities remain intertwined as they did for the Jews, however much people's faiths falter.

A significant number of Jews remain hostile to Western Christianity, as they are not hostile to other religions or to other Christianity. Christian faith endures among Copts, Filipinos, and other Christian peoples and races that nobody blames for the Holocaust.

Neither Jews nor we hold the Caucasus countries of Armenia and Georgia culpable. Armenians know that they are not participants but victims in matters of genocide.

Armenians are a proud people: proud to have been the first Christian nation, proud of their culture, proud of much more. Armenians honour their people and civilisation, as the West so pitifully fails to honour ours. In Armenia, their land, Armenians planted two million trees around a concrete spire reaching to heaven, much as our cathedrals once reached, in memory of their two million dead in the Armenian Genocide. They did not lose faith as the Jews and we lost faith following the Jewish Holocaust. Armenians retain their sense of being a race and a nation.

In the West, building memorials for our race would be nationalistic, insensitive. We now build memorials for everyone else.

Like the Jews, we confine Christian culpability for the Holocaust to the West. We were not there, never killed anyone, but feel complicit in Christian Europe's crime. No longer individuals when guilt consumes us, we are collectively culpable. Our individualism fails to absolve us, but we are trying hard to prevent repetition. Christian guilt is Western guilt, the culpability of Christendom. We are still Christendom after all.

Not merely must we ensure that the Jews not suffer another Holocaust. We must feel the pain.

Ours is collective race and religion like that of other races. All we lack are self-belief and self-affection.

The Church and the Holocaust

Much has been written about the relationship between the Holy See and Nazi Germany, even if little of it is ever read. Our simplistic summary of history is that, with the Soviet Union becoming increasingly murderous and genocidal through the 1930s, the Church in Rome, like democratic Europe, feared the worldwide revolution preached by communism more than we feared fascism. Keeping peace, we appeased Nazi Germany.

In fact, Roman Catholic and Protestant churches opposed the rise of Nazism. With the Nazi regime in power in 1933 and churches in Germany trying to survive, the Holy See and Nazi Germany compromised in a Concordat. It extended previous concordats signed with Prussia and Bavaria.

The Nazis diluted clerical influence on religious instruction in public schools. They curbed the activities of religious schools, while influencing their curricula. Nazis supplanted Christian worship with secular celebrations adopting religious symbols.

Western multiculturalists are much like that today, except that the Nazis glorified the Nazi Party. They worshiped Adolf Hitler.

In 1937, Pope Pius XI issued the encyclical *Mit brennender Sorge* (With Burning Concern), which criticised Nazi philosophy. The Nazis responded with a wave of prosecutions of clergy.

Churches spoke up on behalf of Jews who had converted to Christianity and those married to parishioners, saving some lives, but lacked the cacophony of protest before 1939 that we have come to demand with hindsight. Like the rest of Europe, including most Germans, the Church never imagined the Holocaust.

Jews were not the only subjects of persecution at the time. Fascist Italy outlawed freemasonry in 1925. "Masonry must be destroyed, and masons should have no right to citizenship in Italy," declared Italian dictator Benito Mussolini. "To reach this end all means are good, from the club to the gun, from the breaking of windows to the purifying fire."

Yet, Mussolini could not comprehend Hitler's anti-Semitism; Jews owned shops that Italians frequented. Only under pressure from Hitler did Italy in 1938 finally pass anti-Semitic laws.

Feeling Unforgiven

God forgives us our sins when we repent. We do not forgive us, not since the Holocaust.

We see no value in Christendom, only harm. No other race of a religion is so cruel to itself, its people and past, as are white Christians.

Being Christian that used to bring us pleasure brings pain. Nailing ourselves to angst and principle, white people's last claim that we are races and nations is how awful we are. Consumed by our sinfulness, we are the Church of Christendom's Self-Loathing.

Finding no more than brief peace of mind or good conscience in our suffering and penance, we are consumed by all imaginable guilt for what we have done and think we have done and are doing: before, during, and after the Holocaust. We sinful selves cannot have done more to repent, but it is still not enough. We beg for the forgiveness of Jews, but we need to forgive ourselves.

Ours is Old Testament guilt, Jewish guilt, without the redemption the Crucifixion offered. Western Christianity now leaves us with full buckets of guilt upon which we dwell endlessly, as if Christ did not die to bleed guilt away. He just died.

Absent from our mouths is the joy we should celebrate for being alive and the good deeds we have done: the goodness within us described in the New Testament. There is no command from God to us to perform good works but the sense that performing good works is innate, at least to us.

Pride is a sin. We of the post-Holocaust West think that any sense of feeling good about ourselves is similarly sinful.

It is not. Feeling good for our God-given goodness and for our God-granted forgiveness are not sins. Self-belief is not a sin. Self-affection is not a sin.

God loves us. We do not.

Self-loathing is a sin. It denies God's love and forgiveness. If we do not love ourselves and do not think that God loves us, then others have no reason to like us.

In our pained disposition, shame and guilt have become virtues. Never do Christ's blood, hope, and salvation seem so far away.

Self-Sacrifice

Most profoundly of all, Christianity alone among the major religions on earth made the death and resurrection of our Saviour stand centre stage in our faith. His death for the sins of the world brought redemption and purity again. It is a dramatic conflict between human failing and new-found perfection.

The West has maintained the idea, but without the new-found perfection. Furthermore, sins are now ours alone.

God only forgives sinners who repent of their sins, but we are more self-sacrificing than God. When people of other races wrong us, we forgive them without them repenting for their wrongs.

They might refuse even to admit their wrongs to us. They might boast of them.

The Cross of Christ's death burns in our souls. Other races can be as wretched, corrupt, and pathetic as any sin can be, but we are too stupid and arrogant to think that God or anyone but we can save them.

Self-serving individuals would rather sacrifice each other than sacrifice themselves. Collectively as sacrificial Christendom, we are sacrificing us all.

Only the West conceives that we should hand up our countries, cultures, and races, our churches and parishioners, to aid other races. We cannot conceive anything else.

We never seem more Christ-like than in our capacity for self-sacrifice, but we have redefined what sacrifice should be. Christ sacrificed His life for us. We are not sure why we are dying, we saviours of the world, although we know something about it is good.

Christ's sacrifice was heroic, in spite of His Resurrection. Mortal men and women giving up their race for other races are evil.

The chains of Holocaust bind us. The more millions of people from other races we help, the more millions we feel that we save, but it will never be enough. The Jews who died in the Holocaust are dead. No sacrifice now revives them.

We keep trying to save the world, but it stays mortal, at our mortal and immortal cost. Our racial penitence does not change other peoples' histories.

Christ having given up His life for us means that we do not need to give up our lives so easily, as we now are. We are dying unloved, most notably by ourselves. To serve God saving the world, sensing Him at our shoulders, we need not to die but to endure.

Infant Baptism

Anything less than a world where we all live to the same predictable age with the same health and abilities would be tedious. Our fragility amidst the risk of tragedy adds value and dimension to life.

When death is too soon or too much, we might feel abandoned by God. Christ did on the Cross. We did in the Great War.

Nazi persecution began with requirements that Jews wear the Star of David, so the West became loath to make religion (any more than race) part of a person's identity. Race and religion are much too intertwined, especially for Jews, for our opposition to religious discrimination not to be opposition to racial discrimination, and vice versa.

Religion was not a definition we applied to ourselves or anyone else, not anymore. Religion became private. Our lives became private. We each keep to ourselves. That is individualism.

We ceased foisting religion upon a person at birth, deciding that babies have no religion, nor idiots unable to think. Baptisms are our being born again unto God, but few of the faithful still submit their babies to the baptismal font. Most consider it pointless, that their children decide for themselves when they are old enough whether to hold Christian faith.

Children and adults always had that right to decide whether to hold Christian faith. Calling ourselves Christian might not bring us all into the bosom of God, but it is the belonging of being part of a people. Parents offering their baby children for baptism are declaring that theirs is a Christian family, if not a Christian race. We were Christians by birth, before becoming Christians of faith. We cannot change the circumstances of our birth.

Infant baptism is a rejection of individualism. It is an expression of family and religious heritage, without diminishing a child's rights to decide whether to hold Christian faith.

Christian Upbringing

Christian Western upbringings induct us into Western Civilisation, feeling Christian purely for our race. With knowledge of our religion and God, however dormant, people can find belief in moments of old age, emptiness, or foreboding. They might learn love, joy, or belonging, comprehending a little of eternity to comfort them.

There is no more important idea in the world than the existence of God and that Christ is His Son. There is no decision we make more important than our decisions whether to believe in Him, or lack of decision, every day of our lives. They are our mortality and immortality while we walk the earth.

Mortality does not end us until our bodies die. Our futures after we die depend upon us being Christian. Our futures until then depend upon us being a people.

A person is most likely to take up and keep Christian faith if he or she feels part of a Christian people. Any religious faith is more durable for coming from a sense of being a faithful people in whom to trust, rather than being a solitary person's beliefs left alone.

Belief in Christ that brings us salvation remains a covenant with God unaffected if our faiths later wane. We enjoy eternal lives if, for at least one moment from the first to the last of our lives, we truly believe that Christ is the Son of God and we choose righteousness over evil.

If ever there was a moment through Hitler's tortured childhood, the Great War, or his shattered adulthood thereafter in which he truly believed that Jesus was the Son of God and he chose for that one moment good over bad, then the implications are staggering. For such belief, if ever Hitler held it, in spite of his later actions of such monstrous evil, he enjoys eternal life: his sins washed away on the Cross with the rest of ours. Sin, life, and God are like that.

Mixed Marriages

People identifying with their families do not divide their families by marrying people outside their family identity: their race and religion. Morality depends upon tribalism, making mixed marriages immoral for undermining nationalism and racism, thus morality.

There are no multicultural families. They are multicultural households.

The Bible condones racial and religious discrimination. It also makes it.

Biblical discrimination is often religious. Some Biblical discrimination mixes race and religion, because different races have different religions. Much Biblical discrimination is explicitly racial.

The Hebrew Bible and Old Testament prohibit interracial marriage by the holy race, with some exceptions for related races that we might call close ethnicities. In Judaism, Jews are the holy race.

In Christianity, might all Christian races be holy races? We should not marry with people of other races, Christian or not.

God and Saint Peter entrusted Christianity to the West. Becoming heirs to God's promise means that Europeans were always heirs to God's promise and can never cease being heirs. We are possibly the lost sheep of Israel to whom Jesus was sent. Europeans might be the holy race, even if we lost track of it through the twentieth century.

The Apostle Paul declared Christian Jews and Christian Europeans to be one in Christ, but did not invite them to marry each other. Allowing interracial marriage because God created every race would be like allowing bestiality because God created animals too.

Interracial marriage is blasphemy. Reconciliation with God requires people to send away their foreign wives and mixed-race children.

Within a race, Christians of faith should only marry the faithful. People of religious conviction marry within their religion just as people valuing their cultures marry within their cultures. Otherwise, there is too much they cannot share with their spouse and too much that their children cannot share with both their parents. Their family cohesion suffers.

We are best marrying within our denominations. Parents of the same denomination provide their children a clear denominational identity, with its distinctive sub-culture. Christian denominations are generally ethnic in origin.

Suggesting marriages across religions are more likely to fail does not suit our multicultural vision, even when one spouse converts to the other's religion. It remains anecdotally and intuitively true.

Marriages between people of different religions might be less likely to fail when one spouse holds no religious conviction. Without Western Christianity offering reason to be Christian, the children of mixed marriages are following their other parents' religion, if their biology does not follow for them.

Retaining conviction that Western Christianity has lost, Islam does not recognise marriages with people of other religions. The vanishing West practically demands such marriages, in proof of our religious inclusion: our rejection of Christianity.

Natural Morality

There was no reason for Jesus to detail morality. Recorded in what we call the Old Testament, morality was already clear to people of His time. If any Biblical teaching had been incorrectly communicated through generations or any moral principle misunderstood, Christ could have corrected it. He did not.

Amidst matters of morality recorded there, the Old Testament also described disciplines and practices particular to the region. Most obvious are the rules about food.

The prohibition against eating shellfish was a prohibition against extravagant lifestyles, as it was for the first-century Roman philosopher Pliny the Elder. Shellfish may be eaten where they are commonplace, but extravagant lifestyles remain immoral for being wasteful.

Morals among a people are inapplicable to outsiders. That can be a problem or a privilege.

Compatriots charging each other interest on monetary loans was immoral for exploiting borrowers, but even after clarifying the Biblical prohibition in the Middle Ages, we made a mess of carrying it into effect. Unable to charge each other interest, we declined to lend each other money.

Jews remained free to charge us interest, so became Europe's moneylenders. Instead of resenting each other, we resented Jews.

If God is love because He loves us, then God is science and the scientific method too. Biblical teaching about gender, sexuality, and race reflect our biological natures, with the explanation obvious: God created our biological natures. None of it is arbitrary.

By the early twenty-first century, morality has become offensive in the West. Christianity has become offensive. The morality of other religions would be equally offensive, if we noticed that morality, or were not blaming the West for that morality.

There are those who dismiss traditional teaching (not simply Christian teaching) about race, gender, and sexuality on the basis that we supposedly know more about those fields than people previously knew. Never does arrogance seem more stupid, or stupidity more arrogant. When Christians dismiss Biblical teaching, they claim to know more than God knows.

Western Immorality

With knowledge of God came worshipping God, complying with the moral code set forth in the Bible. Knowledge of God can have no other consequence among good and rational people.

Amidst our rights to pick and choose religion, many atheists and agnostics refuse to recognise God because of His nature or commands with which they disagree, especially commands related to race, gender, and sexuality. Paradoxically, they are more Biblically sound than Christians who simply ignore, interpret away, or edit out those commands. Escaping any innate compulsion to worship God and to follow Biblical teaching requires escaping knowledge of God.

We used to like God being paternalistic, but Western Christians no longer preach. We permit.

In the conflict between God and inclusion, God loses. Love loses. Science loses. We lose.

Politics prevails. Nothing is more important to the vanishing West than diversity, not even salvation.

Unfettered by facts, God becomes someone with whom Western Christians agree. It is our condition upon which we are willing to believe He is real, in the most extraordinary arrogance that human beings have ever displayed.

Christ condemned *porneia*: unnatural and immoral sexual activity. His audiences knew that included anything other than heterosexuality, but Western Christians redefine *porneia* into what we think is unnatural and immoral, which is practically nothing, instead of what God knows to be unnatural and immoral.

The Bible explicitly condemns homosexuality, transvestism, and other aberrations, but still Western Christians believe that God makes some people homosexual or so-called transgendered, because the West now believes that some people are born homosexual or that gender is not biological. It is like saying that God makes some people necrophiliacs, atheists, or Buddhists. Christianity is a religion of choice, but Western Christianity now abrogates personal responsibility, because the ideological West abrogates personal responsibility.

We are not affirming Christianity but individualism: individuals thinking and doing whatever they think and do, however dishonest and destructive. Without nationalism or other tribalism, Christians can be as immoral, unthinking, and dishonourable as anyone else.

Postmodern Christianity

Television programmes that used to be about Christianity became about religion and how stupid Christians of faith can be. While television took to making Christians of faith look bad, it also took to presenting a new form of Christianity, which we tolerated.

For many who do not damn Christianity outright, Western Christianity is no longer a theistic religion. It is a matter of kindness, particularly to them. To be Christian is to be amenable, agreeing with people whatever they say, however heretical.

In our desire to embrace people without Christian faith, we pay great deference to everything they say. We dismiss Christian faith as simply what we have been taught.

Western Christianity became inoffensive. If modernism is the West without faith in being Western and postmodernism is the West without faith in anything, then ours is postmodern Christianity, without faith in being Western or in God.

The Bible advises that we can distinguish Christians from people pretending to be Christian by their love. God and Christianity remain distinct from love, but we have changed the

Biblical statement that God is love from a statement about God (and recognising Christians) into a statement about love: that love alone makes somebody Christian.

In the Bible, circumstances sometimes require God's people to fight. We do not fight.

In the Bible, God's people hate those who hate God. We do not hate.

In the Bible, God's people drive unrepentant wrongdoers away. We welcome them.

When people attack us, we deny that they did. Western Christianity has become naïvety and gullibility, but there is nothing Biblical about naïvety or gullibility.

Our postmodern churches are more postmodern than churches. They are as likely to be parish centres or worship centres: private, personal places, without the authority and togetherness of church.

Instead of the Bible, our postmodern churches often have mission statements, typically less about Christianity than about inclusion. Church doors have always been open to people without Christian faith coming kindly, perhaps respectfully wanting to learn something of God. Today, we welcome homicidal Satanists, but Christians of faith, not so much.

Multicultural Christianity

Since the Holocaust, Christians have become as determined as other white people to protect other races and religions from prejudice. In 2013, Pope Francis canonised the eight hundred and thirteen Italian martyrs of the city of Otranto in 1480. H omitted to mention that they were executed by Turks for refusing to convert to Islam.

Amidst the rising anti-Semitism of the 1930s and especially after the Holocaust, we fused our faith with Judaism in a grand gesture of inclusion. Stressing our Old Testament more than we previously did, we clumsily call our heritage Judeo–Christian, but our Judeo–Christian fusion is neither Jewish nor Christian. The West slowly became a Judeo–European fusion neither Jewish nor European.

Merely because we treat religion in such a passing manner does not mean that other races see their religion, or ours, the same way. Jews had no reason to meld their culture with ours, and every reason not to meld it. Rejecting Christ's divinity, Judaism remains Judaism. Their heritage remains Jewish.

To Jews, we remain Christian, not Judeo–Christian. Jews seeing something good in the West might call the West Judeo–Christian.

The West ultimately fused our faith with every other religion too, but other races do not fuse their religions with ours. No people of religious conviction would.

The tenets of multiculturalism fill the void of our postmodern Christianity. We have succumbed to a Christian multiculturalism, purporting to be part of a single world view.

All cultures are equal. *Ipso facto*, all religions are equal.

Without conviction in Christianity, we are more certain of religious equality than of a Western God. Thus God becomes equally manifest through all religions.

The Otranto martyrs did not think all religions are the same. Neither did the Turks who massacred them.

Western multiculturalism is not about other races and their religions. It is about us: our vision for the world.

We overcome the problems of pluralism with a new religious homogeneity. Rather than letting religion be a barrier to us creating a single world civilisation, Western Christianity becomes a facet of a single world religion, much like any other.

By reducing Christianity to the same as all other religions, we demonstrate our inclusiveness. We let God be any god, but not for any thoughtful philosophy.

Deeming all religions equal is an ideology. It depends upon a complete lack of theological scrutiny and other intellectual analysis. It depends upon emotion, or desperation.

Other cultures do not need any notion of God for us to impute one. Our belief in God includes believing everything else.

Equality commoditises. We commoditise religion.

Refusing to discriminate between religions, we equate prayers of one religion to prayers of another, although few of us still pray. Caring less about our faith than about other faiths, we have reduced religion as we have reduced race: to a universal sameness.

Embracing other religions, we seize upon any hints of commonality between other religions and ours. We ignore the glaring differences between religions or reduce those differences to semantics, as God does not and as people of other races do not. Deeming everyone equally people of God raises people who hate us.

Ours is a multicultural ideology, we have taken up more and more since the Second World War. Ideology has supplanted religion.

Christ-less Christianity

We used to think that our prosperity relative to other races and religions was reason to believe in our God. Deciding that all religions are the same makes their relative poverty another reason for us not to believe in our God.

The failings of other religions become failings of our religion. Doubt in their gods becomes doubt in our God.

People of other races and religions continue to kill and die. When Christians of other races kill, we lament what is happening with Christianity without thought about race. When people of other religions kill or die, we wonder where God is through their crimes and suffering, certain those people are no less people with God in them doing God's will than we are.

God might use people of other religions to further His plans, but installing God in the minds of people not Christian, even hostile to Christianity, is presumptuous, if not absurd. Imposing our multicultural genre upon other cultures is as facile as other fictions in which the ideological West believes.

Christianity becomes a religion without God. In pursuit of our postmodern multicultural ideal, we decided that we were mistaken these past thousand and more years. Without Christ's immortality restored by the Resurrection, the Man our forebears steadfastly called God's Son becomes a nice boy with some nice rules for life: Christendom without Christ.

Christians become mortal beings who live by those rules, although there is no reason to do so. There is no reason to do anything.

Our post-Christian Christianity becomes indistinguishable from the rest of the post-Christian West. Western Christianity becomes much like Western atheism.

Without people of other races and religions needing to ask, we unwind Western Christianity. We surrender our tenets of faith and rites of worship for the sake of inclusion that never was God's.

Nor was it ours, until after the Holocaust.

Religious Nihilism

Having reduced Christianity to love and all religions to being the same, the logical consequence is to denote all religions to be love. We redefine other religions, much as we redefine ours.

Other races do not redefine their religions, although they too can redefine ours. With all that we have done to redefine Christ, people of other religions can redefine Him too, at His and our expense.

There is little, if any, postmodern Judaism like postmodern Christianity. There is no postmodern Islam, except in Western imaginations.

Multicultural religion yearns to be global, but is not global and is not religion. It is Western and it is ideology.

There is no multicultural Islam or Judaism like multicultural Christianity, imagining a single theistic religion for all, but we are too busy embracing those religions to notice. When Muslims are not calling us infidels or worse, they lump us with Jews among the people of the Book. They do not lump us with them.

Neither do Jews. Jews consider only themselves the people of the Book.

What we call our inclusion of other religions, other religions consider our intrusion. Muslims claim that Christians are liars who change our Bibles to deceive Muslims.

They are right. We amend Bibles to remove words we fear might offend Muslims and people of other religions. God does not amend Bibles.

Our relentless efforts to embrace other religions while other religions do not embrace us or each other lead us into irreconcilable confusion. It leads to more conflict.

Multiculturalist ideology declares all religions to be equally valid, but they are also mutually exclusive. The Koran declares that anyone saying that Jesus, the son of Mary, is God cannot be a Muslim.

Christianity believes that God became a man. Islam considers that belief blasphemy.

Christianity believes that Christ was born, died, and rose again.

Sikhism believes that God was neither born nor died, so Jesus cannot be God.

People truly believing their religion cannot believe all religions are alike. If religions mean anything, there are distinctions between them.

Religious inclusion lacks religious conviction. Either Jesus was the Son of God, or He was not. Either Mohammed was Allah's true prophet or he was not.

It is the same contradiction at the core of the nineteenth-century Bahá'í religion, leading to persecution by Muslims for denying Islam. Unlike multicultural Christianity, the Bahá'í religion remains theistic.

If Judaism is right, then Hinduism is wrong. If animism is right, then theism is wrong. It is inescapable for a person of faith in any religion not to believe, however courteously or not, that other religions are wrong.

For all faiths to be equally right or wrong, contradictory as they are, they must all be wrong. The only way to treat contradictory creeds equally, is to reject them all.

Atheism is the only belief system coherent with multiculturalism, but that offends races with theistic religions. Besides, we do not want to be challenged as to what it all means. We get along by never thinking about it.

We believe everything, by which we believe nothing. All peoples are one, we think: all gods and godlessness one. Our only religious conviction is that there can be no conviction.

Beyond atheism and agnosticism, is nothingness: religious nihilism, the end of religion. That is all our globalist vision can be.

Whenever we try to be everything, we become ultimately nothing. Our world without racial distinctions is our West without race, if only without ours. Our world without religious distinctions is our West without religion, if only without ours. Multiculturalism leads us from our one religion through many religions to none.

Other Races' Christianity

Through our age of European empires, Western missionaries stood convinced of the truth of Christianity. The noblest of the noble, they risked their lives and often gave their lives to save other races from damnation.

The great commission, for which saints and others sacrificed their lives in the first centuries after Christ and through the two millennia since then, has been fulfilled. The West spread the word of the risen Lord to all the races on earth. Mission completed.

The Holocaust gave rise to the slander that we imposed Christianity upon other races. We did not. Our mission was not to convert people to God, but to equip them to make choices. Ours is the God of choice.

Races have made their choices. Individuals have too.

Ours is not a Christian loss of religious and other cultural conviction. It is a Western loss. Other races, whether Christian or not, do not think that all religions are the same.

Christianity being our religion does not keep Christianity from being other races' religion too. Christians of other races do not appreciate what the West is doing with their religion, Christianity, but they are not trying to be inclusive. They are not trying to appease.

They remain resolute in their beliefs, clear and unequivocal, without accommodating other religions as Western Christians are. Their devotions are to God and their race and culture, not to everyone else. Their religion they practice with exclusion, as people of conviction do.

Having redefined Christianity to be nothing of note, what used to be Christianity, with devotion to God and trust in the Bible, the West now calls conservative or fundamentalist. In fact, there is no fundamentalist or conservative Christianity.

Nor is there fundamentalist or conservative Islam (as Muslims tell us but we refuse to believe them), Judaism, or any other religion. There is only Christianity, Islam, Judaism, and so forth, with their denominations, sects, and other interpretations all claiming to be true, along with racial and cultural differences.

Some people are devout. Some are not.

The Nature of God

Differences between religions are much more than Jesus' divinity and the Trinity. Values and standards also differ.

The Christian God is very different to Allah. Two very different concepts of the human person emerged. While there is no record that Jesus married, if He did marry, it is inconceivable that He would have beat His wife as Mohammed beat his favourite wife Aisha after she left the house without his permission.

Different concepts of a human person emerged with Christianity and Judaism too, but we put aside those differences after the Holocaust. Soon, we put aside all religious differences.

If we do not redefine Christianity to be without God, we redefine God. We redefine Him in our image, because we have redefined us. We think we are no longer European, but encompass everyone on earth.

We hone in upon God loving the world, discard everything else in the Bible, and decide for ourselves what God should be: what loving must mean. We make Him postmodern, multicultural.

We lower God to our level. We lower Christ.

The God of Joshua was a warrior who conquered cities and slayed their inhabitants. Whatever God was, He still is. He did not change when Jesus was born. Only our understanding of Him did.

We have dismissed the Old Testament to redefine a New Testament without the Old, and without much of the New. Our new visions of God are not Biblical.

Our overarching image of God has become the child's image: a babe in a manger. We dwell upon the meek being blessed and never feel more blessed, becoming less of a shepherd and more of a sacrificial lamb. Not simply meek, we are proud of our meekness, we little individuals.

We have forgotten Christ's righteous indignation and anger, making Him unrecognisable from the Man who evicted wrongdoers from the Temple in Jerusalem. We espouse inclusion and diversity when espousing anything else would make us pariahs, as the Jews made Jesus a pariah. A few days after evicting those wrongdoers, Christ was crucified.

Christ's ministry was radical during His time on earth, but that does not mean we should simply be radical. We should be Christ-like, which might or might not be radical in particular contexts.

Our problem with God is that He has not changed as we changed through the twentieth century. The Christ who will return is no babe in a manger.

The Race of Jesus

Many Europeans lived along the eastern Mediterranean shore through Biblical times. Until the Holocaust, we focused upon them.

Christian Fijians and Africans portray Jesus in their likeness, however plainly He was not of their race. Only we among Christians have come, since the Holocaust, to push Jesus away from our race in our imagery. In our desire to make Jesus Jewish, even mortal, we made Him Middle Eastern.

Multiculturalism strips us of our European heritage. It strips Jesus of being European. We redefined God, and we redefined His Son.

Several races faithfully follow prophets or teachers from other races. Christianity would be unique if our Saviour was of a race that did not recognise Him.

As the people through whom God first revealed Himself to the world, the Israelites were unique. A confederation of tribes, possibly twelve, they shared the Old Testament cultural stream, and little else.

Being tribes and clans descended from Jacob and other Abrahamic lineage might have been metaphorical. Could the tribes of Israel have been different races? Which among them might be the holy race?

Kind David was descended from Ruth, a Gentile. David was ruddy, which is to have a fresh reddish complexion or possibly red hair. It can only describe a European, such as a Galatian Celt.

The Biblical sons of Zion were brighter than snow and whiter than milk, their bodies more ruddy than rubies. God's people never appeared more European.

There are no Biblical descriptions of Jesus, although other descriptions from that era point to a European Christ. Along with David and other Old Testament figures, Jesus might not have been racially a Jew, as we understand Jews.

On His human side, we know nothing of the Virgin Mary's race. Might she have been Celtic? Her race was Jesus' race.

The Bible distinguishes Israelites from Jews. All Jews were Israelites but not all Israelites were Jews. Samaritans, including the famous Good Samaritan, for example, were Israelites but not Jews.

Christ too could have been an Israelite without being a Jew.

Christ could have been Caucasian.

The Jews were more synonymous with the Hebrews. Israel and Judah were separate kingdoms, which might or might not have united for a period. In etymological origins, the Jews were members of the southern Kingdom of Judah, including the tribe of Judah, from which the word "Jew" came and which in time absorbed remnants of other tribes. The Jews of today are generally descended from the Kingdom of Judah.

Judaism was not codified into writing, the Mishnah and rest of the Talmud, until about *anno Domini* 200 and 500: After Christ. Jesus might not have been raised religiously a Jew, so much as raised according to our Old Testament origins.

While a Samaritan woman called Jesus a Jew and others called Him king of the Jews, Jesus did not call Himself a Jew. Jesus's own words suggest He was not a Jew, referring to Jews as if He was not one, in spite of the Davidic line being of the tribe of Judah and thus Jesus being of the tribe of Judah by paternal, earthly lineage.

While Jews hated the tax collectors, Jesus ate and drank with them. Jews opposed paying tributes to Romans and other earthly beings for defying their single God, but Jesus told Jews to give unto Caesar what was Caesar's and to give unto God what was God's.

Deferring to the Roman Empire in everything except religion, Jesus' command to love thy enemies and persecutors was a command to the Jews to love the Romans. It was not a command to us to love our enemies.

Christ on the Cross pleaded for the Romans' forgiveness. They knew not what they were doing.

Christ was the God for Rome. Perhaps He was not obviously born of one Caucasian race so He could be Saviour to all. That would not make Him any less the Saviour of the world.

The White Christian Burden

For all our similarities, there are differences between Christians in churches and their counterparts outside. Churchgoers are more engaged with civic life, as churches are. They are generally more generous, more helpful, and nicer.

Atheists and agnostics accompanying their Christian spouses to church might become nicer people for being part of a Christian community. Alternatively, they might already be nicer people, to have Christian spouses and accompany those spouses to church. Christians without faith are nicer in Christian communities than otherwise.

Western generosities are never more evident than under church angel wings. They make our failings most obvious.

Our forebears expended great wealth glorifying God, building beautiful churches, cathedrals, and basilicas, but we have become like Judas chastising Jesus: chastising our forebears for supposedly wasting resources to glorify Him. We proudly prefer to give everything away.

White people have become individuals. We no longer provide for each other. We provide for everyone else.

More weights in our white man's burden, Western churchgoers are no less engrossed than other white people with saving strangers in faraway places at the expense of our own. We do not imagine confining our charity to Christians any more than we imagine confining our charity to our race. We might even like our beneficiaries being of other races and religions, for what we think it says about us. We persist helping them whatever they think of us, and whatever we think of ourselves.

Whether we credit our prosperity to God and providence or not, we think God wants us to share our wealth with the world. He does not.

The Bible espouses loyalty, not disloyalty, to our families, races, and religion. While acknowledging there will always be poor people, commands to help the poor and needy are the poor and needy among a people and fellow Christians. It does not cross religious lines.

This is not financial equality, but charity. There is no general Biblical sharing: no general Biblical equality.

From the time of the Disciples onward, some Christians have been able to give up all they owned because they lived among donors and donees sharing a common identity. Racism and other tribalism afforded them mutual responsibilities to provide for each other.

Without tribal connection, our munificence to other races and their religions simply adds to their sense of entitlement. The arrogance of our good works evangelism imagines our example quietly turning a few appreciative others towards God, converting some of them to Christianity, when their races long ago chose otherwise.

The Bible does not tolerate passengers or parasites. We do.

While our money helps other races and their religions, the logs in our eyes are much bigger than any specks in theirs. Our churchgoers' benevolence in deed and spirit can seem boundless, but with each Christian charity's resources finite, every beneficiary from another race or religion is one less from ours.

Saving Everyone Else

Centuries ago, France was the Eldest Daughter of the Roman Catholic Church. Today, her churches are boarded up and derelict. What stirred with great hymns have become hollows in still air.

Our remaining churches are often reclusive, disappearing. If they dream of reaching up to heaven as our churches once reached, they are not reaching very far. Not quite ashamed, they are not confident either. They are trying just to survive, fearing the consequences if they reveal themselves.

Losing our countries erodes God's house on earth, but we do not dwell upon losing so many from our race who could have had faith had our countries endured, but who live and die unsaved. We are the only race on earth more interested in promoting our religion among other races than trying to keep our people on board.

Instead of saving the West, we save everyone else. Saving souls, but not ours, the absent Church evangelises elsewhere, while the faiths of white people falls.

We are preoccupied with preaching to other races, although we lack the conviction to say very much. We are too polite to proselytise.

Western church missionaries are much like faithless Western aid agencies, helping and entertaining the impoverished of other races instead of our poor. We trip around their countries teaching school, building homes, and caring for their sick.

As if that were reason to do so, we think that opening our lands to other races improves their chances of becoming Christians. Our affluence might tempt them, much as primitive people seeing the material wealth of Europeans with our missionaries formed cargo cult religious movements. We equate material desire with spiritual desire in them because we do in us.

Their alleged conversions to Christianity might last no longer after they obtain refugee status or residency permits than do those of prisoners in gaols with high dispositions to finding God, before facing parole boards. We equate repentance with regret: regret for having been caught.

Other races do not enthuse about lost white people adopting their religions as we enthuse for the few from other races claiming ours. Desperate for new believers, we are keen to champion them coming from other faiths or from none; we do not discriminate. They are crude recruits, but better than none, while our race stays away.

Other People's Churches

Everyone needs God. Only some of us realise it.

Western Christianity survived communism better than we are surviving individualism. We are not surviving multiculturalism at all.

Individuals do not care. We observe, whatever our faith.

We no longer join churches because we no longer join communities. Other races fill places of worship because they retain their senses of family, race, and nation: community.

Thus they also retain their respect for authority, if only their own. Respect for authority has become much rarer among us, especially for our own.

Communities within churches are like those without. When other races go to church, they prefer the company of their own.

Without our collective identities but with great deference to other races' collective identities, we accommodate their desires to be together that we would not allow for ourselves. White congregations would have welcomed immigrants to join them in church, but immigrants prefer services and whole churches reserved to their race, much as they confine their countries and communities to their race.

Immigrants sitting beside us do not remain when opportunities to be with their race arise. They do not do so outside churches, or inside churches.

Without loyalty to our race, we evict the last members of aged white congregations to make way for immigrants. Church congregations move seamlessly from our race to other races, without us noticing the change. If we notice it, we welcome it, much as we do with our countries.

Christianity becomes a donut faith, flourishing among some of the races to whom we took it, dying among ours. Whether Christianity blossoms among other races or they simply take the venues we give them and meld any little of our ritual they like with their senses of togetherness and authority is not clear. We are just letting our religion fare a little better among them than it fares among us.

Church and State

To escape some of the complications that Thomas Jefferson saw in Europe (particularly France), another new idea that he espoused for the Virginia colony and then the American nation was to separate Church and state. It was a separation of structure protecting each from the other, ensuring that Christians of all denominations were equally eligible for public office.

The first Europeans in Europe to separate Church and state were the French. Roman Catholicism ceased to be the state religion with the 1789 revolution.

The French Revolution rejected Christianity in favour of the so-called Cult of Reason. Maximilien Robespierre tried to install a new state religion: the Cult of the Supreme Being. Both failed, before being banned in 1802.

Roman Catholicism was again the state religion through various imperial periods of the nineteenth century. Church and state were not formally separated until 1905.

The 1918 communist Russian constitution separated Church and state *"in order to ensure...freedom of conscience."* The 1924 communist constitution of the multicultural Union of Soviet Socialist Republics did not separate Church and state. The 1936 Soviet constitution separated Church and state as well as Church from schools, in a distinction of which we have lost track in the West.

Separating Church and state is not law in most countries, not even in the West. In the United Kingdom, the Church is the state. The reigning monarch, the Defender of the Faith, heads the Church of England.

Britain prohibited Roman Catholics and their spouses ascending to the throne, but never thought to prohibit people of other races and religions when those races and religions were unimaginable among European royalty. The most practical effect of Britain's official state religion being the Church of England is in the designation of public holidays.

Campaigning in 1960 to become America's first Roman Catholic president, John Kennedy cited the separation of Church and state to assure Protestants that he would not be subject to the Pope instead of the American people. Kennedy embraced Roman Catholics, Protestants, and Jews, as America's religious pluralism always had. Only after the Holocaust, did we think that embracing Jews required us to wind back Christianity.

Significant among the people determined to separate Church and state in America, especially as regards schools, were Jews. Once content for the countries in which they lived to be Christian, Jews ceased to be so content after the Holocaust.

We also ceased to be so content. While other races continue presuming that religion relates to all things, we separate Church and state as an article of faith, even where there is no formal legal separation. It is postmodern dogma, when we are so determinedly postmodern.

Western states melded with multiculturalism, becoming defender of that faith. Separating Church and state now keeps Christians in check. No longer allowing Christians of all denominations into public office, separating Church and state now prefers no Christians in public office.

If separating Church and state does not exclude the faithful from office, we must leave our faiths behind. While the West pursues peaceful coexistence between religions, we are not looking for coexistence with Christianity. The West's solution to conflict between Christians of faith and the faithless is to demand submission from the faithful. Other religions are not so angrily dismissed from debate.

Secularity

When our countries and races were Christian, other people's religions did not offend us. We simply did not believe them.

Christianity did not offend people of other religions. They simply did not believe it.

With multiculturalism and our endless indulgence of other races and cultures, Christianity has come to offend people of another religion. It has come to offend people without religion.

While Western Christianity has become unimportant, other religions remain important. When we talk up one immigrant religion in the name of multiculturalism, adherents to other immigrant religions demand the same, but there are too many religions for us to field. Rather than omit a religion leaving its adherents feeling excluded, we exclude them all. We remove religion altogether.

The best possible outcome for our religious pluralism, the only way not to offend, becomes silence. None of us say anything. So much as harbouring thoughts towards God are better not mentioned.

All religions offend secularity: a polite word for prohibiting religion. Secularity becomes atheistic evangelism, or evangelical atheism, when it prevents people practicing their religion. When Western churches advocate secularism, they deny Christianity.

Simply because we came to deem religion a private personal affair, does not mean that other races agree. Like our forefathers and mothers, the rest of the world does not treat religion as something so personal it should be hidden away. Religion fills people's lives, as it once filled ours. They are not as reticent as we are to call upon God.

Outside the irreligious West, people feel the state should express religion because people express religion. Secular states separate political leaders from religious leaders and thus government from the most pious, but they do not separate politics from religion.

Muslims expect Muslim countries to honour Allah. Jews of faith expect Israel to honour their god, although they might debate what their god demands.

Nobody expects Western countries to honour God, but we used to expect it. We used to expect our churches to defend us.

Other races' religious bodies still defend their races and countries. Western churches defend their races and countries too.

Oaths and Pledges

We can hardly expect people of other religions to put Western countries ahead of their religions when, increasingly since World War II, we have not put our countries ahead of our private little religions: our religious individualism. We who once pledged our loyalties to God and Country no longer do.

For people believing in neither God nor Country, there is no problem with pledges to both because neither pledge means anything. Nor is there a problem for people believing in one but not the other, because the pledges to the other mean nothing.

For people believing their religion and in their country, along with people sincere in the pledges they make, there is a risk of conflict. Any religiously pluralistic country sets up a conflict between allegiances to religion and to country. Any religiously pluralistic group sets up a risk of conflict between allegiances to religion and to the group.

Any pledge made collectively by a religiously plural group of people, as the multiculturalist West tries to be, either omits God and religions altogether or reduces all religions to subjective personal beliefs, each as credible as any other. Religious relativism means that we each have our own truths, each religion its truth. There are no facts about God, or very much else.

Multiculturalism makes religion fickle, coming as it does without the imprimatur of a nation or race but only the murmur of private opinions. To call our faith mere beliefs alike other faiths lacks conviction that our faith is true. They are words for non-believers. Religious equivalence makes no religion real.

Our multiculturalist oaths often talk of respect. Whatever respect means, it does not mean worship or faith. It never did.

What remains are each person's transient arrays of whatever abstractions he or she wants, for as long as he or she wants them. People speak of beliefs as if they have always believed them, but with each new belief they forget what they previously believed.

Doing away with oaths to God and Country, however expressed, leads ultimately to oaths by which people are true to themselves. They are not oaths but declarations that people will do as they please. The only person to serve is me. That is individualism.

When our countries were Christian, God and Country were the same loyalties. By not having both, the West ends up with neither.

Christian Education

Since the Second World War, so-called civil libertarians have set about denying the West our liberties: our rights to religion, to practice our religion in public, to congregate together, to a country. Never before have the liberties of so few been wielded to deny liberties to so many. The more we have liberties under God and Country, the fewer our liberties under multiculturalism.

Other people's liberties prevail over our liberties. Any government reach into schools became a means to deny our children a Christian education: to expel Christianity.

Other races strip Christianity from our schools because Christianity is not their heritage. We strip Christianity from the West because it is our heritage.

Cultural sensitivities do not remove all hints of Christianity from our educational and other institutions. Christianity comes out of hiding to be assaulted.

The Torah commands Jews not to use the Lord God's name in vain. When Jews complain "Jesus," they declare Jesus not to be God. Anyone complaining "Jesus" does the same.

If people dare mention Christ, they do so to reject Him. Multiculturalism means we tolerate contempt for Christianity unimaginable about other faiths. When we treat our religious heritage with disdain, we invite other races to do so as well.

Multiculturalism means the onus is upon parents to teach their children at home their religious and other cultural heritage. Parents of other races teach their children the faiths of their forebears, but Western parents have too much else to do to drop our children at Sunday school each week.

Not only Christians of faith might want Christian educations for their children at school. So might atheists and agnostics, when their heritage is Christian.

A traditional Christian education gives children reason to

wonder. It teaches children and then adults the questions to ask about life, God, and the universe when they are ready to ask. It teaches them eternity.

It is education about churches and other Christian features of our culture. It informs children of the good works churches do helping poor people and other traditional Christian precepts, such as caring for the weak, distrusting materialism, cherishing the environment, and standing up against corruption.

Creative minds should escape endless activity, taking time to imagine and contemplate. Biblical stories are our children's birthright.

So-called libertarians are not satisfied with their right to join hell. They demand the right to bring others along for the ride.

Atheism and Agnosticism

The primary purpose of Christianity for the West was knowledge. Pursuing truth and believing in facts, our European ancestors adopted Christianity because they knew it was true.

Atheism and agnosticism are Jewish and Western inventions, born of knowledge of the Abrahamic God. People born to religions without theism struggle to be atheist or agnostic because they do not know the belief they reject or about which they are uncertain.

Among Europeans, atheism and agnosticism come from our Christian questioning. They are consequences of the choices God grants us whether to believe in Him. Christian nations allow people freedom to choose whether to be Christian.

Judaism does not have that tradition of choice, but does have a tradition of Jewish obedience or disobedience to their god. Jewish atheism and agnosticism are disobedience. They are also a rejection of something from their cultural heritage, if not their cultural heritage altogether.

Rarely are we keener for civil liberties than when it comes to atheists espousing atheism. When atheists deny Western children a Christian education and upbringing, they deny children their opportunity to choose what to think: their chances for faith or rejection of faith. Atheists denying others the knowledge to make up their minds about God lack the intellectual rigour to argue their atheism. Rather than win debates, they avert them.

People need to know something to reject it as much as to believe it. Uninformed choice is no choice at all.

Freedom of religion or irreligious thought requires knowledge of religion. Whatever their heritage, only people knowledgeable about religion can discuss it. Without knowledge, we are simply indifferent.

If we do not teach our children about Christianity, our children will have no comprehension of God. If Western Christians do not assert our faith, the West will lose all comprehension of God. Unable to form views about matters they do not know, people will not know enough to be atheist or agnostic.

Religion at Work

Following Napoleon's defeat at Waterloo in 1815, the Kingdom of Prussia took control of the Rhineland. In an early instance of unnatural selection, a rabbi's son Hirschel Levi converted to Lutheran Christianity so he could continue working as a lawyer in Trier. He also changed his name to Heinrich Marx.

Like others saying what his audience wants to hear to get what he wants, the conversion lacked conviction. In spite of being baptised in 1824, Marx's son Karl grew up in a home without religion, and became the primary figure in the development of atheistic communism.

When religion was important, Christians and Jews preferred to work and deal with people of their religion. Christians preferred working with Christians of their denomination.

Late in the twentieth century, religious discrimination became wrong in the West. Western businesses prohibited talk of religion, ostensibly to avoid religious division.

We have more reasons than that to keep our faith to ourselves. We have our careers to consider.

Traditional religions contemplate something other than money motivating people to act, unlike our mass media advertisements. Religions offer joy from something other than shopping malls or holidays in expensive resorts. They speak of contentment (even salvation), without hunger to work and to spend.

Being religious can mean lacking ambition. We are not putting the company first.

Ours is the Age of Ideology, the Age of Money. God is simply not on board.

Economic Religion

Superseding differences between religions requires superseding religion, unless another religion supersedes all others. There has never been a culture without something describable as religion: affording people purpose, structure, and comfort beyond the mechanics of food, clothing, and shelter, satisfying our needs to believe in something bigger than us.

Even irreligious ideologies do not allow the vacuum of there being no religion. Communists do not lump their ideology with archaic notions of religion, but theirs became an atheistic religion.

With the failure of communism, our multicultural vision needed something else to replace Christianity. Commerce was our first hope to supersede differences between religions, as it was between Christians and Jews. Our unfettered individualism created commercial religion, as we needed it to do.

Without Christianity to keep us, capitalism (as much as communism) became a religion for atheists. It is all economics, political or not.

A company is a legal entity potentially immortal. The omnipotent economy is God the Parent, whose child is each self-worshiping individual: mortal me. Ours is a holy duopoly, trying to mould us in its image. The economy is a jealous god.

Commercial hegemony is the things that we buy, paid for by what we sell, even if all we sell is our time at the office. Employees and consumers adhere to a system of values: free market economics of supply and demand. Employers embrace employees sharing their beliefs, whatever those employees' physical or mental attributes. We find in our times our quests for success, without dwelling too much upon what success means: a job title and business expansion? Telling each other they are all that we need, we trust the company brochures.

We do not want one Bible but expect a consumer-driven choice of management textbooks, often titled with a metaphor about animals. Faithless sceptics do not understand.

Our new Western faith is not in God. It is in human resources departments.

Marketing replaced the Messiah. Our places of work are our places of worship.

We replaced the birth of one saviour with the periodic return of another. Santa Claus might have been inspired by the Christian bishop Saint Nicholas giving presents to good children, but he has long left Christianity to become patron saint of the post-Christian West.

The more children believe in Santa, whatever the faiths of their families, the greater the expectations imposed on mummy and daddy, auntie and uncle, grandma and grandpa. There are no judgements or morality, no offending anyone by deciding that he or she has been bad, just presents. Where there are presents, there is purchasing.

There is thus great irony in some pious Christians objecting to Santa as a distraction from the Biblical essence of Christmas. By speaking to commerce, Santa survives. When people realise that Santa is Western Christianity's last muttering, he is restricted, or banned.

While Christmas becomes shopping for gifts, Easter becomes shopping for food. Western rule is not by God, but by mammon. We do not need church when the stores are awash with religion to eat.

All religions being the same, we also reduce Islam to a matter of shopping. Muslims do not, but we do.

While the West now finds Christian faith offensive, practicing Muslims and Jews might object more to the pervasiveness of commercialism. No religion ever promoted self-indulgence as wantonly as commercial advertising does.

Spirituality

Ancient Greek philosophers unfurled the idea that we have souls. We of the West still sensed our souls freely only a generation or two ago. We also knew body and wondered what mind and heart might mean.

Since then, fewer and fewer of us reveal our souls to ourselves or each other, suggesting that our souls are not surviving through our isolation, our individualism. Instead, we have ideology, work, and shopping. Souls need society.

Better than we still sense ancient souls in ourselves, we imagine them in other races. Those souls might not be there.

The multiculturalist West's failure to provide religious conviction does not just leave people with little reason to believe our religion. It leaves people vulnerable to other religions, with the right marketing.

There is no greater misnomer than claiming that ours is an age of science. For all our assertions of science, multiculturalism commands that we respect other religions, however ridiculous they are. The more ludicrous the belief, the ruder it becomes to challenge it. Ours is an age without science.

If we believe anything aside from ideologies, it is typically an undefined, uncertain, personal plaything we call spirituality: anything ephemeral outside the physical and immediately practical. Mere spirituality can be religion for display: an ornamental motif. It might be interest in personality, character, or values. It can be no more than a means of politely respecting all religions without believing any religion. Everyone should be pleased and no one offended.

Spirituality comes without morality telling people what to do and not do. If it did, consumers would not select it. Biblical preaching is much too prescriptive.

White people want spirituality to help us feel good, legitimising ourselves in our lifestyles and lives. Spirituality comes without conscience or command, except as a reason to do whatever we would have done anyway. Anything else, we refuse.

Money is never far away. What we want, we can buy.

Spirituality for purchase is more of a transaction than simply dropping anonymous money into a church offertory plate. All the trappings of Christianity we can find in our spiritual free markets: free market prophecy, free market communion, a universe to buy.

Customers are not buying truth but belief, equating perception to fact. We can believe that we control the universe or believe that nobody controls it; whatever we want to believe. Without any more questioning than the rest of our continuous consumption, we feel what we want to feel. Hope, meaning, and destiny become self-fulfilling promises.

Our smorgasbord of religions is commercial. Never are cultural and economic forces more connected.

Wherever there is spirituality for sale, there are sellers earning money. Astrologers offering good times to come are never more than a phone call away, charging by the half minute. Religion for sale entertains.

Mere spirituality for professional people is normally a little self-centric meditation, led by a paid consultant. Christian meditation dwelt upon God, but the individualist West prefers spiritual individualism, focusing already self-absorbed minds even more on our individual selves and careers.

Claiming spirituality while eschewing theistic religion does not take people closer to God, but God is not where the vanishing West is trying to go. Each spiritual loner sits alone amidst a revolving universe, believing whatever he or she bought to believe. In our nihilistic individualism, we worry about everything and care about nothing.

The contrast between religious lives and lives without religion is never more striking than in the moments of our passing. Little wonder that families without religious faith are dispensing with funerals altogether.

As the French writer Voltaire lay on his deathbed, a priest asked him to turn back to God and renounce the Devil. "Sirs," Voltaire reputedly replied, "this is no time to be making new enemies."

The West readying for our deathbed has much the same approach. Voltaire at least believed there was a god.

Sport

The Greek god Zeus' statue at Olympia was one of the seven wonders of the ancient world. Ancient Olympic Games were festivals celebrating Zeus, with arts and theatre as well as sport.

Every four years, the Games suspended conflict between Greek states. Each state's glory otherwise bought with blood was instead bought with sport.

Sports were part of Western cultures, played with passion while spectators pondered. When we had countries and cultures, good health, fun, and honour mattered more than merely winning.

Communist Karl Marx described religion as the "*opium of the people*," comforting the exploited and impoverished peasantry. The illusion of happiness distracted peasants from demanding the communism they needed to achieve real happiness.

Sport is the opium of our postmodern West. It allows acutely private people to discuss and debate something other than work, food, and wine, without risking relationships being formed in a workplace any more than a stadium. Sport affords us every emotion denied us in the rest of our lives. Refusing to discuss politics or religion for fear of the conflict, we argue vehemently about sport.

Never is a workplace more tribal than when employees don company tee shirts to play against teams representing other employers, but employment has become too capricious to sustain company tribalism. Professional teams are more enduring. Without race or nation, any beloved team can be a person's identity.

Sports are more market economics, and not just for the television subscriptions and for jerseys emblazoned with sponsors' logos. We barrack for teams owned by rich magnates as if our membership dues or season ticket makes a team ours, and even without memberships or tickets.

Consumers buy the best value and discard the rest. Success is part of the purchase. Our loyalty is often no more than applause, from good-weather admirers who boo our team losing.

Ours is sport without exercise. Sports fans do not need to play sport, unless our career is playing sport. People who play sport normally talk less about it, unless they are paid to commentate.

Sportspeople are what Western employers think employees should be, with a total commitment to their employer winning. Sportsmen are postmodern gladiators: battles for people spared fighting real wars. Sports are the wars in which nobody dies.

Like David against Goliath, there is bravery, if only for a ball. Fans feel a little like William Tell or Robin Hood each time their heroes fight.

Sport is a rare situation in which nations still mean anything in the West. More than merely a word on a form, we accept, encourage, and even expect sporting loyalty to our citizenry as we do not tolerate nationalism otherwise. We cheer with compatriots who, a day later, we would let die in the street.

Countries again become tribal, with national selection warranting loyalty in the West that race and religion no longer do, with all thoughts of nation but none about race. An American whose kin come forever from Ireland will support an American Pakistani sportsman playing an Irishman. Tiny tiers of loyalty they might be, but any short loyalty is better than none.

Like other vestiges of human identity, marketers tap into patriotism if it helps sell their sports. When patriotism risks profit, it is discarded.

Fans cheer and abuse players who, like us, take the best-paying jobs they can get. If a person's business is playing, then for more money or a better chance at winning a championship, he will transfer from one team to another.

She will transfer from one country to another. A professional sportswoman can represent one country and live where she likes.

For all our supposed sports nationalism, we still cheer competitors from other races. It proves we are not racist.

Another ploy of our politics, sportspeople are model heroes and heroines for what we think heroes and heroines should be, especially when they are from other races. Sports express our post-racial vision.

Uniforms affirm that most important of traits to the postmodern West: equality. We see the colours of jerseys, but not of the players, except when we laud the diversity. Physical features endure only when performance related.

Races other than ours are not as superficial as we have become. Whatever their citizenship, they are as loyal to their race playing sport as they are loyal everywhere else. Sport does not build the belonging between races and religions that the West imagines it does. The only sport that matters, if any sport matters, is the sport that people we care about play.

A Multicultural Inquisition

Medieval Inquisitions sought to remove heresies from Christian teaching and practice. The Spanish Inquisition weeded out Muslim and Jewish influences among Moors and Jews who had converted to Christianity, as well as among Spaniards after centuries of Muslim rule. Inquisitors restored Christianity.

Our New Western Inquisition is a Multicultural Inquisition, weeding out Christian influence. We prefer derision to trials and execution.

Ours are the countries that our forebears built and defended by God, but that we do not defend. Since the Holocaust, we have feared that Christianity disturbs pupils and people of other religions.

Western Christians tolerate atheism and other religions. Encouraged by our meekness, atheists and people of other religions are not so tolerant of Western Christianity.

Not that we care. Caring would be rude.

The obliteration of Western cultures by multiculturalism is never starker than it is in relation to religion. Multiculturalism has supplanted Christianity.

More dogmatic and intolerant of other creeds than Christianity ever was, multiculturalism has become our new Western religion: faith for our new global vision. In multiculturalism, we trust.

Dismantling even our calendar, dates before Christ, B.C., become B.C.E., replacing Christ with the Common or Current Era, whatever that is. We are no longer *anno Domini*.

Multiculturalism makes Christianity offensive. Rather than immigrants feeling excluded by the sight or sound of our Christian heritage, we feel excluded.

Our determination to accommodate other races and their religions while riding roughshod over ours means that it is hard not to feel the West is at war with Christianity. If not the West, then another race or races is at war with Christianity, for being at war with the West.

The Religion that Hides

As we do, citizens of the Soviet Union treasured their rights. The 1936 constitution allowed freedom of religious worship and anti-religious propaganda. Anti-religious propaganda abounded, while religion was secreted away.

By 1982, we thought that communism had all but eradicated Christianity from Russia. At the funeral of general secretary Leonid Brezhnev, the most powerful man in the Soviet Union, his widow bent over Brezhnev's body, kissed his forehead, and dabbed her tears away with a handkerchief. Their daughter kissed his face twice, before his coffin was closed.

The quiet, moving moment was the final ritual of the Russian

Orthodox Church, in marked contrast with the political theatre around it. Religion is always more moving than politics.

In 1982, Russia represented the cruel communist empire suppressing people wherever it reached. Our free West appeared to be the beacon of freedom.

Early in the twenty-first century, that has all turned around. Russia is one of the few beacons among European peoples. Her restored Christianity and rest of her culture might well be less than they were before the Great War and coming of communism, but they are more than most of the West retains.

For most of the West, Christianity has become religious fanaticism, for maintaining morality amidst individualism and for not submitting to other religions amidst multiculturalism. Christianity should be shut out of sight.

Like the old Soviet Union, our right to anti-religious propaganda prevails over any right to religion. We are free to denigrate Christianity. We are not free to defend it.

Our freedom of religion is a freedom to be silent, to worship in private a faith we keep secret. Other people's religions are not our concern. Our religion is nobody's interest.

Christianity was never less public than it is under multiculturalism. Western welcoming of other cultures drives our cultures into hiding.

Still, Christianity bubbles beneath the new Western watch. We quarantine religion, as other races do not, sealing our customs peculiar to our people in private homes and churches, where people walking past cannot see them. We confine our Christianity to close chapel walls and the insides of our heads, where the rest of us are not supposed to look.

We have lost our nexus to religious expression, even if we choose to participate. Western Christians imagine maintaining our faith apart from our culture, but religious meaning and body come from practices along with beliefs. The West is losing both.

The Universal Declaration of Human Rights in 1948 expressly extended rights to religious worship to both private and public places, but human rights are for other races' benefit, not ours. We are supposedly so powerful in the present as not to need them and so wicked in the past as not to warrant them. We defend and advance other races' religious rights, when salvaging ours might discomfort them.

Ours is the religion that hides. Christianity might be fading fast from the West or dying altogether, but we cannot see enough or hear enough to know.

Our Lands of Other Faiths

Religion became unimportant when the West dropped Christian conviction, clarity, and Biblical definition. Imagining all religions being the same means there is hardly any reason to bother being Christian. Nothingness Christianity offers people no reason to believe.

With Western churches espousing diversity and inclusion, Christianity wanes. If churches are not following God's natural laws, the faithful have little reason to remain. The faithless have little reason to come.

At best, ours is a pan-religious Christianity, and our numbers are falling. At worst, we are of another religion altogether. Being of no religion is something in between. None of them provide salvation, although we think they all do, for the sake of inclusion.

When the West renounced Christianity and the rest of Western Civilisation, we left spaces to be filled. Our religious vacuum invites other races to consume us with their religions.

Self-belief prevails over self-doubt. Self-doubt prevails over self-loathing.

Religions offering certainty and belonging flourish. The collective convictions of other races in their religions are more persuasive than the flimsy resolves of individual white Christians. Conviction prevails over confusion.

When the West turns our minds to religion, we care less about the faith of our forebears than the faiths of other people's forebears. With our confidence in other cultures, the religions we teach our children are other races' religions.

Atheists do not challenge other races their religions as they challenge us our Christianity. That would be culturally insensitive.

Mere mention of Christianity to people of other religions we consider culturally insensitive, but us participating in their prayers and religious rituals we feel gives us new perspectives. It gives us their perspectives.

We do more than respect other religions. Instead of learning about other people's religions knowing that they are other people's religions, we publicly affirm them as we refuse to affirm our religion.

We do not need to know those other religions to affirm them. We do not try to understand them.

Muslims still believe Islam. So can we.

Our faith is in multiculturalism: in people and religions not ours. The West embraces without question other races' religions for no other reason than that they are other races' religions.

Karma

The open West is an answer to prayer, but they are other people's prayers. We recite other races' prayers and mantras as we no longer recite our forebears' prayers or sing our forebears' hymns.

From our smorgasbord of religions and bits of religions, karma is among our most popular selections. It offers meaning without structures and discipline: godlike without godly rules. We decide what is nice and what is not. Karma affirms us: each of us.

In a lovely construct of the universe, karma lets us construe rewards when we want affirmation of whatever we are doing or have done. We do not incur punishments, but can see suffering in other people's lives when we want to condemn them. It is individual self-interest, cloaked in the guise of some kind of spiritual belief: a reason for self-centred individuals to be nice in the expectation we will benefit, without attempting to fathom why we should.

Belief in karma does not make people nice. It assures people that they already are nice, and that people they do not like are not nice.

Our faith is not in karma. It is in each individual us, but not collectively us. We do not wonder how karma could possibly be real.

Asian identities remain their races, undiminished by their religion. No Buddhist nationalism crosses Asian racial lines.

For Western devotees without racial identities, Buddhism is more than another mantra. Buddhist nationalism is for white people. Without race, it is all white Buddhists have.

Holy Mothers

God choosing the Virgin Mary to bear His Holy Child made Mary the Holy Mother: holy by reason of being that mother. Joseph was not the Holy Child's father in the ordinary sense, but theirs were the earthly lines to which the Holy Child was born.

Roman Catholic churches remain distinctive for their glorious white statues and other representations of the maternal Holy Mother. Paintings of the feminine Madonna and Child are among the most beautiful fifteenth and sixteenth-century Renaissance artworks: exquisitely warm and fond affections. Her Baby boldly boyish but vulnerable, they loved and would uphold the other.

Deference to Mary is deference to motherhood. Celebrating Mary celebrates motherhood.

When the Western Christmas lost its Christian story, we lost the instant in history when the universe centred upon a single birth. We lost the power and magnificence of infancy.

A man does not need to be Christian to recognise that a woman producing his child is a goddess, if only to him. He has every reason to adore her.

Men and women of a race or other tribe recognise the mothers among them to be goddesses to all of them. They all have reason to adore mothers among them.

The reverence for motherhood that Protestants diminished with the Reformation, the West lost with individualism. We who once venerated parenthood no longer do.

The West did not need to lose our love for childbearing because we lost our Christianity. We lost it anyway.

There is nothing Biblical about losing a life to celibacy, as monks, nuns, and Roman Catholic clergy do. Those erring Christians aside, people of faith bear more children than people without faith. Western Christians do not bear enough.

Within all races, the religious bear more children than the irreligious, but fewer white people than people of other races retain religion. Removing our religion reduced our childbearing.

Religious people bearing more children do not make the vanishing West warm to religion, not ours anyway. It is another reason to reject religion.

Higher birth rates among Muslims have allowed Islam to overtake Roman Catholicism as the largest religious denomination on earth. In the tally not just of faiths but people, we are losing.

God does not dissipate without Christians, but faiths disappear without the faithful. All in all, the post-Holocaust West imagines there would be less conflict if Christianity and the rest of our cultures abated. White people abating produce the same result.

Armageddon

The Bible foretells Armageddon. Poor peasants cannot afford to worry about it. Rich people want something to fear.

Persistent fear reflects a lack of faith in us to deal with a danger. It reflects a lack of faith in God that He would subject us to danger with which we are unable to deal.

Looking for Armageddon in all the wrong places, since World War II we have feared a cold war, hot war, coming ice age, computer failure, global warming, climate change, our over-population, and viruses. About the only things we refuse to fear are other races and religions, not since the Holocaust.

Armageddon bubbles unnoticed towards us. We might not know the meaning of God's Revelations to John until after the events they describe happen, for their purpose is not to provide us clues as to when Armageddon is coming as might a detective mystery novel provide clues as to a culprit's identity. The meaning of each Revelation might be clear looking back afterwards, although by then we might be too busy worshipping Christ returned to look back at anything.

Those Revelations' purpose is simply that the story begun in Genesis will end, heralding a new story. Details matter less than there being an end, of sorts, before the next eon. What is allegory and what is real does not matter, although might matter when each prophecy unfolds.

That might not be for thousands of years. It might be sooner.

Until then, God allows us a degree of dominion over mortal earth. Biblical prophecy was a vision. It was not a command.

Conservation

The West has a long history of conserving and caring for our natural environment. Like us, lush green forests and waterways were beautiful. We wanted fresh water to wash around our mouths, clean air for our soft lungs to breathe. Bright red robins and sprightly brown squirrels were joys to behold.

We kept our neighbourhoods beautiful. Our collective and individual self-interests were intrinsically rational and reasonable.

Marxism, on the other hand, dismissed environmental concerns for being bourgeois. Communist governments cherished factories spewing pollution into the air and water.

The free West kept factories away from people. We insisted that industry operate as cleanly as it could.

The economics that compels so much of the West does not deter us from spending money on the environment. The West is more likely to preserve species than erase them.

White people cannot bring ourselves to cast ill upon other races or to feel good about ours, but no race on earth does more than we do to protect the environment. It is hard to see most of the world doing much at all.

Most other races pollute more than we pollute. Those that pollute less than we pollute also produce much less.

We used to care for the environment because we cared about people. We have come to conserve the natural environment oblivious to whether anyone enjoys it. The less and less we protect our people, the more and more we protect trees and animals.

Environmentalism

Without nationalism or other tribalism, white people's interests are the world on one hand and our individual selves on the other, without much beyond or between. In the choice between the environment and other people, other people come second, even our children.

We progressed, in the language we like to employ, from environmental conservation into strict environmentalism: ideological environmentalism. Without gods or God of one's own, the next big thing for the post-Christian West is a galactic environment.

Postmodernism does not pertain to environmental issues. There is no relativism but only facts, unquestionable and absolute. It is our prefect crusade, providing new-found certainty and conviction with the zeal of old-world missionaries among the unwashed.

Ideological environmentalism is in the nature of religion, reflecting our religious heritage we remember, even own, but no longer practice. For all our talk of liberty, we want limits upon endless liberties. We desperately want disciplines: the structures of society. The West's comprehensive embracing of environmentalism affirms our need for religion of some form or another.

People who refuse to countenance societies, parents, or God suggesting what they do, faithfully accede to the pronouncements of people and bodies declaring the environment their mission: a sort of environmental infallibility. They trustingly accept without question the dictate of an undefined, omnipotent, and omnipresent Mother Earth, as revealed through her environmental prophets.

Ideological environmentalism brings us little pleasure, in spite of our feelings of moral superiority and other self-righteousness. It comes with senses of obligation and sacrifice.

The sacrificing fools are sincere, while the hypocrites gain. They enjoy the moral superiority and other self-righteousness without suffering. They live well while harming the environment, according to their edicts.

The purpose of environmentalism is not to help the environment. It is to comfort people into thinking they are helping the environment. It is to give people something in which to believe and a sense that their life has a purpose: to save the planet.

Environmentalism is a multiculturalist perspective, ideal for a West that rejects nations, race, and traditional religions. We think globally, and nothing is more global than the environment, short of God. We do not want God.

Especially for people uninterested in economics, environmentalism fulfils our Western dream of a single world religion superseding traditional religions, with a particular liking for the most primitive peoples. While demanding that white people progress in political and ideological terms, we laud primitive peoples who have never progressed.

Indigenous environmentalism advances their tribes, while rejecting the West. So does Western environmentalism, never far from the rest of our self-loathing.

The presumption of civilisations is to prosper, but no longer are we trying to sustain Western Civilisation. The dream of our vanishing West is biodegradability, trying to be inconsequential. We want no evidence of our presence, even a lowly turning of leaves on a lonely forest floor.

Climate Change

Like our other postmodern religions, environmentalism draws upon our religious heritage. Environmentalism offers eternity, or something towards it: interests after we die. People who could not care less about the day after tomorrow fret themselves silly about sea levels in seven hundred years' time.

Science we dismissed when it comes to human biology, we cite over and over to support the environment. Scientists are important again, when they are climate scientists. At least since the 1980s, their modelling has prophesied all manner of doom because of the carbon that industries emit into the atmosphere.

They prophesied global warming, but that did not happen. Then, they recast their prophecy as climate change. They could hardly help but be correct, finding affirmation in every weather event and from every lack of a weather event.

Those scientists still kept erring in their prophecies. They and their followers remained unfazed.

Whether human activity affects climate and, if so, the extent of those effects should be a question of scientific discovery, analysis, and debate. It is not. It is science as a matter of faith.

We do not need all scientists to agree. We need them to say they agree.

Shutting down our industrial and agricultural capacity because we no longer need them would be rational. Doing so when we still need them is irrational.

More often than not, climate change sceptics are people old enough to have witnessed the politicisation of knowledge. We have seen facts about race, gender, and sexuality replaced by ideologies masquerading as science. We have watched the world we lived through replaced by an historical narrative unrelated to historical reality. We have enough confidence in people, well some people at any rate, to know that we can deal with changes to weather.

So, we pay little credence to what we are told is a scientific consensus. We might have met sceptical scientists, whose apparently well-researched and well-reasoned papers remain unpublished because journals and universities refuse to publish dissident viewpoints about anything important. We might know of the scientists privately admitting they do not agree with the consensus, but whose research and other funding depends upon them saying publicly they do.

All sides agree climate changes. The West has lost confidence in our capacity to deal with it.

Conversely, we are certain the weather is within our control, according ourselves the role we no longer give God. What were acts of God became acts of us.

It is our arrogance to think that we could save a planet. It is our despair to decide that we are already destroying it.

Instead of being a quest for knowledge, climate change is another edict by which people prove their environmentalist credentials. We are happy to frighten each other about environmental issues, while we refuse to worry about other races and religions.

Voluntary Western Extinction

To ease environmental pressure, environmental concerns should cap immigration, but that would be nationalist. With our globalist mindset, environmental concerns should also move us to try to cap the populations of people most rapidly procreating, wherever they live in the world, but that would be racist.

Instead, we curtail births among us, who are already contracting. Unlike other religions, our all-consuming Western environmentalism discourages childbearing.

Environmentalism expresses our racial self-loathing when we see ourselves purely as environmental costs and burdens. We have reason not just to stop growing, but to vanish.

Ideological environmentalism comes not from respect for our race, but contempt. It comes not from belief in God granting us dominion over the earth to enjoy and protect, but from rejection of God and of us being here at all.

Intrinsic to our post-Holocaust West is the same relentless sense within us: cowering to bleaker tones instead of what could be shining bliss. In spite of our bravado, central to our Western weak hearts lies hopelessness. There is hopelessness about the weather or our fixation with it, along with much more. Some of us try to improve things, but most feel we do not have a chance. Amidst all that we call upon ourselves to bear, ours is the era no longer of war and holocaust but of futility.

Thus we shut down Western Civilisation and become childless, suffering through another grand sacrifice to save Mother Earth, while excusing other races from action. Other races emit more carbon than we emit, but we fearmongers insist the West's gesture will inspire other races to go some way towards doing the same, although our other grand gestures for globalism have not inspired them to ruin themselves too.

It is our white man's burden never heavier. It is our saviour complex never more martyring.

Ideological environmentalism is another option to erase Western races and civilisation for the supposed sake of a planet that does not notice we exist. It is another expression of hostility and even warfare against the West, by people refusing to admit they are party to war.

Only the vanishing West imagines purpose to a universe without our descendants in it. Other races value their environments and might fear climate change, but they are not sacrificing themselves to save us or anyone else. They are not as prepared as we are fatalistically to fade.

So we satisfy ourselves with the pleasure of letting the West die. We are martyrs in the best tradition of Christ.

Ideological environmentalism is not just a religion. It is a suicide cult.

Where Jesus was once our inspiration, the self-appointed reverend Jim Jones now stands in His place. If the West is a village, the village is Jonestown.

Voluntary Human Extinction

Without racism, Western self-loathing becomes human self-loathing. When we want other races to shut down and become childless too, our ideological environmentalism expresses our human self-loathing. Our avowed globalism and self-hatred compound the other.

We complain that people consume agricultural and mineral resources, as if agricultural and mineral resources are not there to be consumed. Obsessing with climate, we reduce human existence to the emission of carbon dioxide. People have become pollutants: toxins of an environment of which we no longer feel we are part.

Environmental concerns that make us curtail populations of people do not make us curtail populations of pets. An earth filled with forests needs only animals to produce the carbon dioxide that plants breathe. Without people, animals enjoy all the oxygen. Plants and animals have more water.

Instead of seeing paradise in nature encompassing our beautiful selves, Western environmentalism sees paradise without us: nirvana for no one to see. Stripped of self-respect, we are less important than lichen.

We consider ourselves worse than all the plagues God inflicted upon Egypt, or would if we knew anything of our cultural heritage. If we are not lauding everyone else with our cries for diversity, we are damning us all with our cries of human-made doom.

Causes that could have valued people above all else have become corrupted into more ways of making people disappear. We no longer love nature because we love people, but because we despise people.

We hate human beings, but that was the same humanless splendour from which dinosaurs and other species became extinct before humans appeared. Species have constantly evolved and become extinct on this planet quite apart from anything that human beings do. The only difference between those species becoming extinct and our vanishing West is the voluntariness of our demise.

Yet with more carbon in the atmosphere, plants flourish. With more plants there is more oxygen. We too flourish, on a self-correcting planet, if we are willing to stay.

Instead, we pursue oblivion believing oblivion will benefit plants, animals, and rocks. Saving the beetles and plankton, ours is human sacrifice: our own. Bugs and birds we yearn to save can break through our fading flesh as we invite them to do, gnawing at the calluses we do not realise are ours.

The post-Christian West is sin without redemption, in spite of our best labours: sacrifice without resurrection. It is the earth in desperate darkness at the point of Christ's harrowing, cruel death:

the curtain in the Temple torn. It is the earth again waiting the news of that first Easter morning: the Resurrection and redemption.

Christian Europe valued human life in honour of God who granted us life. No longer believing in afterlife leaves us willing to lose the last life we have left. If there is reason in people not bearing children for the sake of the planet, there is reason for them leaping straight to their deaths.

Christian Faith

Without nationalism or other tribalism, we are alone through the universe. Without God, we are alone through eternity.

Belief that Jesus Christ is the Son of God flows from essentially two streams of reasoning. The first is deductive, beginning with the universe and the astonishing sophistication and complexity of life.

The more we experience the natural environment with people in mind, the more we believe in science and God. Believing that God created everything is far more credible than thinking that everything simply arose or was always here. God is the best explanation for everything continuing as it does. Of all the theistic and polytheistic religions, the loving God that sent Jesus Christ is the most credible.

The second stream of reasoning is inductive. It begins with the Nazarene Jesus.

His Resurrection so convinced His Apostles and other followers that what He had said through His ministry was true that they gave their lives to spread and defend the word of His divinity. History accords many inspirational people, but no other person inspired as He inspired. People honoured Him not because anyone compelled them to honour Him, but in the face of every earthly persecution compelling them to abandon Him.

Atheism requires a greater leap of faith than does Christianity. Agnosticism is giving up without decision.

Multiculturalism requires the greatest of all leaps of faith. It dismisses reams of historical and current evidence about race, religion, and other culture, especially those of racial, religious, and other cultural conflicts.

The Crusades

When foreigners threaten Europe in the twenty-first century, Western churches welcome those foreigners. When marauding Muslim Seljuk Turks from Persia threatened Europe from the eleventh century, the Church sent Crusaders to defend us.

The first Crusade began in 1095 under Pope Urban II. The last Crusade ended in 1272. We blame the Crusades upon religion, but only upon Christianity, because we are told the Crusades were unprovoked Christian aggression against peaceful Muslims at home.

They were not. The Crusades were our response to Turks conquering the Armenian capital in 1064 and the rest of Armenia in 1067. Turks conquered Jerusalem in 1065 where they massacred three thousand Christians, destroying churches or making them stables. Their defeat of Christian Europe at Manzikert in 1071 threatened the whole Byzantine Empire.

When Emperor Alexius I, a Greek, pleaded for help from his fellow Europeans, we did not condemn his intolerance. We helped.

Franks were the most numerous of Crusaders, but the Crusades were a pan-European movement. They came from upper and lower classes in the commonality that race and religion were. Most Crusaders were men, some were women. Legend holds that in 1212, French and German children began Crusades. With piety and pilgrimage, we set forth to liberate Christ's holy places and protect European peoples.

Our ancestors were heroes and heroines. We are told they were villains. The falsified Crusades make Muslim and that other Semitic immigration, the Jews, into Europe seem fair. They are not.

The Crusades were a glorious failure. While we might know that they failed, we are unaware of the Muslim invasions that inspired them.

We are equally unaware that Muslims subsequently evicted Europeans from what became their land. The Mamluks vowed to cleanse the Middle East of Franks, massacring or enslaving the last of them in 1291. It was much like Adolf Hitler trying to cleanse Europe of Jews, except the Mamluks succeeded.

Late in the twentieth century, Turks, Arabs, and other Muslims did not care what happened eight hundred and more years earlier in battles that Muslims ultimately won, until we cared so much. By our unfounded shame for our past, we encourage and empower other races and religions to sharpen their swords against us.

Christian Walls

Most of us keep to our comfortable ecclesiastical corners with people with whom we concur, but not German priest Martin Luther. Early in the sixteenth century, for all the good deeds the Roman Catholic Church did, Luther took to task those in the Church who had abandoned Scripture in favour of selling Papal indulgences. Today, Luther could chastise those in the Church corrupting Christianity in favour of multiculturalism, diversity, and other heresies.

We of the faith presume that we do not need saving. We do.

Christendom wanes, but will only end if we allow it to end. If we are not sitting idly by waiting for another Luther to rise and a sort of Reformation II, or Restoration, we had better be Luther ourselves.

The Bible speaks to borders. Before nation states, there were city states, around which God allowed walls in people's defence. Towns secured by walls and iron bars prospered.

Destruction of the walls, as occurred at Jericho, represented the defeat and destruction of a people. Nehemiah repaired the broken wall around Jerusalem, because men and women of God secured themselves and their people with walls.

Also defending her borders and people was the Roman Catholic Church, before multiculturalism. Following the sacking of the old St Peter's Basilica by Muslim Saracens in 846, Pope Leo IV commissioned the building of the Leonine Wall encircling Vatican Hill.

We did and thought all manner of things before multiculturalism, which we no longer do or think. When churches abandon Scripture, they abandon God. They abandon people. Any church working against her people does not deserve to survive.

Christian Nationalism

God's commands make sense. Our post-Holocaust Western

interpretations of them do not.

Christian expressions of goodness remain fine values for Christian communities, but only within Christian communities. Sharing makes no sense with people who do not share in return.

The Apostle Paul's oneness in Christ was Christian nationalism, between Christians of different races in the face of Roman persecution. It did not encompass people who had not become Christians.

Christian, Muslim, Jewish, and Hindu nationalism are natural expressions of Christianity, Islam, Judaism, and Hinduism. Religious nationalism, whatever the religion, supplements but remains secondary to race and nation. Where national and racial interests diverge, religious nationalism fails.

Turning the other cheek to people who harm us makes no sense towards self-serving individuals, people of other religions, or people of other races. Different nations might be equally Christian, but Christ commands nationalism for each. A kingdom divided against itself cannot stand, whatever the kingdom.

Nationalism does not require love or Christian conviction, but love and Christian conviction command nationalism and other tribalism: honouring our mothers, fathers, and other ancestors; taking precautions to protect our compatriots; making provisions to protect our descendants. If Western individualists who have sanctimoniously rejected racial loyalty need people to protect them, they will need to call upon the white nationalists they despise.

Jesus' parable of the Good Samaritan demonstrates that our generosity should be towards people with whom we disagree. Their modern-day equivalents are not people from other races but, for example, the dissidents we condemn among our own.

There will be no great re-emergence of Western Christianity without Western Christians to lead it. We will not revive religion or the rest of Western Civilisation, let alone be a light again for the rest of the world, without recovering our collective identities: our best sense of being races and nations, of being Christendom. We will not be Christian peoples again without being peoples again.

While ever enough of our race survives to be a population, God's relationship with our forebears gives Him a reason to save us, provided we do all that we can do to save ourselves. Our ancestors were not willing to give up on us. Neither is God.

3. AIDING ISLAM

Simply because we separate ourselves from our cultural heritage does not encourage other races to separate themselves from their cultural heritages. Western churches rewriting Scripture for the sake of diversity do not inspire other races to rewrite their religious teachings.

Races other than ours retain their self-belief. There remains nothing more natural than them defending their religions and other cultures.

To the extent that they can, they assert their races and cultures wherever they live, inside their countries and outside. Their cultural self-confidence inspires it. Their religion might require it.

Our failure to defend our cultures invites other races to assert their cultures ever more so. Our lack of self-belief only enhances their self-confidence.

They may well have contempt for our cultures. We do. Immigrants treat us with contempt no worse than we treat ourselves: our race and cultures.

Unconcerned about offending us, immigrant races do not simply demand that we relax and abandon our traditional rules and cultural norms to accommodate them. Knowing they can never offend us, they increasingly demand that we submit to their rules and norms. With responsibility upon us to make multiculturalism work, we keenly comply.

Why would any immigrant race not demand of us everything it can? Even if it does not succeed immediately, it suffers nothing by its demands from the tolerant West.

We keep raising other races' expectations of the extent to which we will indulge them. Soon enough, refusing their persistent demands makes us feel mean. It makes us feel bigoted. The compromises of today become the injustices of tomorrow.

Other races value their cultures enough to want their cultures to prevail not just in their homelands but also in the countries in which they now live: those countries that used to be ours, but that we tell them are now theirs. By insisting that our cultures not dominate because our cultures are ours, we invite immigrant cultures to dominate because they are theirs. Caring about the future of Western Civilisation becomes culturally insensitive to people of other races.

When its numbers are large enough, any immigrant race or league of races will decide the extent to which it imposes its rules and other cultures upon us and our descendants. Immigrants will want laws protecting their families and faithful from what they regard as corrupting influences, even if we individualists do not want protection for our families and faithful. Those corrupting influences are much more than just Western multiculturalism, gender fantasies, and sexual depravity.

Diversity is for the West. No other race wants it.

The inevitable outcome of multiculturalism is our submission to self-confident collective peoples. Multiculturalism is a phase along the way from Western races and cultures to other races and cultures.

It is one thing for a race to choose a new religion. Only the vanishing West invites other races to impose their religions upon us.

This is not merely the immigrants' doing. It is our doing. We allow it. The most self-certain collective religion on earth is Islam.

Imperial Turkey

Founded about 660 B.C., the Greek city of Byzantium in Anatolia became Constantinople and the eastern capital of the Roman Empire in *anno Domini* 330. For a thousand years, it stood as a centre of Christianity and Classical Greek people and culture.

When Muslim Turks invaded their way into Europe, the boundaries of Europe and of pan-Europe narrowed. Geography does not make a person European.

Turks captured Constantinople in 1453 and the last of the Eastern Roman Empire fell. If that seems a long time ago, it was less than seventy years before Spain conquered the Aztec Empire and only a century and a half before British settlement of the Americas began.

Constantinople is now Istanbul, as if it never was Greek. The

Greek and Roman cities of Troy lie in ruin, now in Turkey.

Turks replaced Greeks, Romans, and other Europeans. Turkey replaced Anatolia. Islam replaced Christianity.

The sixth-century St Sophia Church had been the largest church in the Eastern Roman Empire and the largest interior space of any building on earth. After the fall of Constantinople, it became a mosque. Demonstrating Turkish government secularity in 1935, the uneasy juxtaposition of one religion in another religion's place became a museum.

At the turn of the twenty-first century, that museum could have been as much a monument for multiculturalism as Christian Europe, in our expectation of what Europe might become through mass Muslim immigration. Ours would be deconsecrated Christian relics in scattered European cultural enclaves, while Islam rules peacefully over us.

While we with our cultures withdrew, other races increasingly asserted themselves and their cultures. Unconcerned by meek Western objections, Turkey converted the St Sophia Church museum to the massive Hagia Sophia mosque in 2020, to the cries of "*Allahu Akbar!*"

No longer is the St Sophia Church a Christian relic. No longer is it a European cultural enclave.

Originating in the fourth century, the Church of the Holy Saviour in Chora became a mosque during the Ottoman era of the sixteenth century. It became a museum in 1945 and a mosque again in 2020.

At least those buildings survived. Later in 2020, Turkish authorities demolished what had been the nineteenth-century St Georgios Church known as the Hagia Sophia of Bursa, functioning variously over the years as a church, mosque, and cultural centre. In recent years, having been forbidden from any use but Muslim worship, it had fallen into ruin.

Multiculturalism was a phase along the way from being Greek and Christian to being Turkish and Muslim. If Europe is a church, it is St Sophia.

While the West makes our lands multicultural, other races make multicultural lands theirs. At the beginning of the twentieth century, twenty percent of Turkey's population was Christian. A hundred years later, it is a hundredth of that.

There is every reason to expect a growing Muslim population to make St Paul's Cathedral and Westminster Abbey into museums, before making them into mosques. A West made psychologically incapable of distinguishing one race or religion from another will celebrate the mosques for reviving traditions and culture as if the traditions and culture were ours, pleased if those relics are not demolished.

Islamisation

At some time through its history, every Christian, Muslim, and Buddhist race became so. Countries and even empires have undergone religious transformations.

Races and ethnic groups became Christian as a matter of choice: religious self-determination. We did.

Some races and ethnic groups might have become Muslim voluntarily, at least at its introduction, through trade with Arabs. Conquest compelled others to become Muslim. Islamisation refers to the processes by which tribes, countries, or races become Muslim.

There is no equivalent word for tribes, countries, or races becoming Christian. We cannot imagine that happening anymore.

Rarely does one monotheistic religion replace another, but it has happened. Albania was a Christian country from 325. Slavic history was more complex, but Slavs became Christian and in the Balkans emerged the Christian Bosnians.

In the fifteenth century, conquest by the Ottoman Turks subordinated Europeans to Turks, but Europeans could acquire equality with Turks by becoming Muslim. Over time, Albanians and Bosnians did.

Turkish persecution of Christian Albanians, Bosnians, and others in the Balkans included the punitive taxes normally imposed by Muslim authorities upon people of other religions. It also included the Ottoman Empire's child levy or blood tax known as devshirme. From at least as early as 1438, Turks enslaved Christian Balkan boys aged from eight to sometimes as old as twenty. Some Christian Albanians and Bosnians courting favour with their rulers gave up their sons voluntarily.

The Turks forcibly converted those boys to Islam, whereby the boys ceased being slaves. Any prohibition on slavery in Islam only prohibits slavery of fellow Muslims.

From the fifteenth to the seventeenth century, Turks trained the newly Muslim boys in Istanbul to be soldiers and officials. They went onto become most of the Ottoman Empire's provincial governors, military commanders, and senior government officials. The practice effectively ceased in 1648, because Turks came to prefer training their sons for those roles.

Reviving its nationalism gave rise to an Albanian renaissance from the late eighteenth century into the nineteenth century, but the Ottoman Turks retained their imperial oversight. Albanians did not revive their Christianity as they revived other features of their culture.

The Austro–Hungarian Empire ended Turkish occupation of Bosnia in 1878. Europeans did not compel people to become Christian, not even to return to being Christian.

Russia also weakened the Ottoman Turks, letting nationalism resurge throughout the Balkans. Albania declared its independence in 1912.

Europeans evicted the invasive Turks from the Balkans, but have not evicted them from Europe. Turkey remains in occupation of Anatolia.

Most races have enjoyed choosing the lands they occupy and incurred other races making choices for them. We only complain when Europeans choose.

The End of the Cold War

Some people oppose ideologies because they know the damage those ideologies do to their people and cultures. Thus Afghans fought their communist regime after a bloody communist coup d'état in Afghanistan in 1978.

Other people oppose ideologies because they have ideologies of their own. Through the Cold War from 1947, the individualist West arm-wrestled the communist Soviet Union.

When the Soviet Union invaded Afghanistan in 1979 to prop up the communist regime, Afghans and other Muslims fought the Russians for being invaders. We aided the Afghans because they fought communists. America provided more than twenty billion dollars to train and arm Afghan resistance groups, pursuant to

Operation Cyclone and the Reagan Doctrine.

The mutual threat from communism made Muslims our allies, we thought. When the battered Soviet Union withdrew from Afghanistan in 1988 and '89, continuing Soviet military aid kept the communist regime in place until 1992.

The Cold War ended in 1991. Communism ceased threatening us.

In 1993, American Japanese political economist Francis Fukuyama (married to a white American, Laura Holmgren) argued that political and economic conflict was over, Western liberalism had prevailed over communism, and there would become, in effect, a single world civilisation. It was Hegelian dualism reminiscent of Karl Marx and his conviction that history ended with communism.

Like communism, it was also globalism, enthusiastically dispensing with races and cultures. Having brought on board someone from another race can only have added to our sense of certainty.

American political scientist Samuel Huntington rejected Fukuyama's thesis. He warned of the world returning to the cultural clashes it had experienced before the ideological conflicts of the twentieth century.

Since the Great War, ideology had masked racial and cultural conflicts for the West. What Huntington forecast were explicit ethnic, racial, and cultural conflicts, like those that had already broken out in the formerly communist Yugoslavia.

Removing our ideological masks might have allowed the West to side again with our race instead of neglecting it. We could have defended our religion and rest of our cultures instead of discarding them.

With the end of the Cold War, conflicts explicitly around capitalism and communism between European peoples had passed, at least for a while. Our Age of Ideology had not, if only for regions of the West that geography had spared from suffering communism.

Individualism remains. Multiculturalism remains.

Serbia

Foremost among our new ideological enemies through the 1990s was little Christian Serbia, one of the impoverished Eastern European countries recently liberated from communism and among the Balkan countries reborn from the dissolution of Yugoslavia. Serbs were kinder to each other and to strangers than were we in the individualist West by 1993, but her new-found nationalism made Serbia a Western pariah.

The Great War began in 1914 with Russia, France, and Britain defending nationalist Serbia from Austria–Hungary and Germany, in what was an internal Austro–Hungarian Empire affair. By the end of that century, we had no currency with Christian Serbia defending herself from Muslim Bosnians and Albanians, in internal Serbian and former Yugoslavian affairs.

Bosnians and Albanians were no less nationalist than were Serbs, but we allowed them their nationalism. They were Muslim.

Also in 1993, British journalist Ed Vulliamy wrote of being with Muslim Bosnians fighting Christian Serbs. "*My father had the honour of fighting fascism; I instead have the strange privilege of meeting the people who are fighting a pale but unmistakable imitation of the Third Reich.*"

We called the Serbs fascists, for being white, Christian, and nationalist. Serbs did not call themselves fascists.

Serbia was socialist. The ruling Socialist Party of Serbia had been renamed from the old League of Communists of Serbia, with a long history fighting fascists, including the real Third Reich.

Forty-eight years after Nazi Germany's defeat, we wanted the war we thought our fathers and grandfathers fought, having redefined World War II into a war that our fathers and grandfathers would not have recognised. We wanted to fight the white Christian nationalists we wish Britain had fought before 1939, oblivious to our fathers and grandfathers having been, like the Serbs, white Christian nationalists.

We presume to hate war, but war was never our fear. If war had been our fear in the immediate aftermath of each world war, it was no longer our fear by 1993.

American journalist Chris Hedges also covered the conflicts in the crumbling Yugoslavia. "*Many of us, restless and unfulfilled, see no supreme worth in our lives,*" he wrote in his 2002 book *War Is a Force That Gives Us Meaning,* "*...war, at least gives a sense that we can rise above our smallness and divisiveness.*"

When we lost our racial loyalties, we did not stop harming white people. We stopped saving them.

Multiculturalism at War

The most common prayers the West pleas are for peace. Come Christmas and Easter, with more reason than ever to dwell upon God, life, and death, our messages are peace. The dove is the symbol we set forth to the world. We are the gentlest people on earth.

Just not with each other. The most striking feature of the world is not that there should be racial or religious combat but that, where it embroils white people, we have become so quick to fight for, not against, other races and religions. We buy into battles to battle our own.

We are still fighting wars, but not as we used to fight and as other races still fight. We are the siblings at arms, but armed against each other still believing, or again believing, in their nation, race, or collective Christianity, and thus in ours.

From 1995, Serbs had to contend with insurgency within their borders by Muslim residents of her Serbian province of Kosovo. Calling them Kosovars made them seem like locals instead of immigrants, but the criminals, terrorists, and revolutionaries of the Kosovo Liberation Army were racially Albanians. We wanted them free to stay within Serbian borders fighting to secede from Serbia, rather than fleeing the fighting to return to Albania.

Both sides committed wrongs in the cruel Kosovo war erupting in 1998, as happens in war. Our eyes were upon Serbs, not Albanians.

Britain's prime minister Tony Blair championed a new type of war. Being the humanitarians we are, we called it humanitarian war, as if there was anything humanitarian about it.

The war spun less from a British sense of fair play (even without racial or religious loyalty) than from Blair's devotion to multiculturalism. Being British, we are still the world's policemen, but we are no longer as nice to white Christians as we are to everyone else.

America's Albright Doctrine also employed military force for supposedly moral objectives, as if morality required her to fight white Christian nationalists. Secretary of State Madeleine Albright was three-quarters Jewish.

Albright was among the foreign ministers at a conference in London in 1998 debating the Serbian action in Kosovo, when her aide Jamie Rubin suggested she might accept the soft language threatening the Serbs that had been suggested by the French and Italian ministers. "Where do you think we are," she retorted, "Munich?" In the 1938 Munich Agreement, Britain, France, and Italy averted war by allowing Nazi Germany to annex portions of Czechoslovakia in which ethnic Germans lived.

This new kind of war was simply resuming, or continuing, an old war: World War II, revisited in our multicultural vision. We are fighting World War II as if it were not yet won: fighting each other as if the other were a dictator who died and regime that ended in 1945.

With what we devotedly call our ideals, German Greens replaced their slogan of "No more wars," with "No more Auschwitz." Believing in a world without boundaries, it is hard to think of any other reason to fight, but we love to fight.

In 1999, America, Britain, and our allies bombed Serbia to support Kosovars. It was civil war in Christendom: a wilful war waged against a European people, dropping bombs upon intolerance no longer of Jews but of Muslim crime and terror.

Niš had been the birthplace of Constantine, the first Roman emperor to convert to Christianity. In 1999, Dutch aircraft dropped cluster bombs on Niš, killing Christian Serb civilians.

If bombing Serbia was a "battle between good and evil, between civilisation and barbarity," as Blair claimed in a speech in Chicago, then we were evil. We were the barbarians.

Quicker to fight Serbia than we fought Nazi Germany, we fought as fervently as our forebears fought, but not to save Europe, at least for Europeans. We fought to save others from Europe. Aiding Kosovars by killing Serbs by the hundreds, we felt prouder than we had felt for generations.

When bombs proved inadequate to force Serbian troop withdrawal from her province, we threatened invasion. Serbian troops withdrew.

The Kosovars then expelled Serbs and other racial and religious minorities from Kosovo, but we did not intervene to save Serbs. We are too preoccupied with white peoples' intolerance to notice what other races do.

We are unconcerned about the races and religions we embolden by our actions, wishing we had been unconcerned about communism when we did not fight Nazi Germany during the

1930s for fear of communism. We are far more fearful of Europe's prejudice, and far more vengeful towards it, than we fear other races' prejudices against us. We have lost the concept of any race or culture but our own being a danger.

The Iron Boot of Multiculturalism

Another former republic of Yugoslavia was Macedonia. Like Serbia, nationalism meant Macedonians were kind to strangers. They retained, or found again, strong moral codes that we in the individualist West were losing, but prostitution, crime, and corruption were among the moral breakdown that came with encroaching individualism.

Ethnic Albanians moved with arrogance aloof from Macedonians, except to rob them. Albanians formed a mafia in Macedonia at least as bad as the Sicilian crime families in Italy.

By 2001, Albanians in Macedonia had also become terrorists. Suffering a similar, albeit smaller, conflict than Serbia, several hundred people died in fighting between Macedonians and Albanians. Whenever the Macedonians surrounded a group of terrorists in a village, American authorities telephoned the Macedonian leadership and threatened to bomb Macedonia if Macedonia attacked the Albanians. Having seen the killing in Serbia, the Macedonians backed down.

If totalitarianism is the use of force to impose an oppressor's will upon others, then multiculturalism had become totalitarian. Enforcing racial and religious diversity in Europe, we expected Serbs and Macedonians to tolerate crime and terror by other races and religions, as we tolerate them. We refuse to respond with commensurate force, or even just prejudice, however many of our people die. So should Serbs and Macedonians.

We demanded that Serbs and Macedonians treat Albanians as individuals with individual rights. A contradiction it might be, but we punished Serbs collectively when they did not. We threatened to punish Macedonians collectively if they did not.

Bosnians and Albanians were never our allies. We bombed Serbia and threatened Macedonia because we hate white intolerance so much.

The only altruistic reason for people to risk their lives

protecting others is nationalism or other tribalism. When people are being killed, war against a people's nationalism is war against that people.

Rarely has a Western government since World War II defended her people, countries, and cultures as the Serbian and Macedonian governments sought to do. Instead, we submit our citizens to the world, certain of the justice we do. We live for our new global ideal we value above each other's lives, consequently our lives.

Wars have not stopped because we stopped defending ourselves. Without racism and nationalism, Western governments have proven willing to let us die, even kill us. Rather than fight other races and their religions in our defence, we will bash our own to the death.

Other People's Wars

Imagining our British forebears who fought Nazi Germany also fighting Christian Serbs or Macedonians in support of Muslim Bosnians or Albanians is fanciful. Nevertheless, by the end of the twentieth century, we were certain they would have.

In a sense, far behind their patriotic duties to God and Empire and through the long alliances of war, our slightly more distant British forebears fought for Serbia in 1914, when her foe was Austria–Hungary. Had our forebears from either world war been drawn to war in 1999, they would have fought for their fellow Christian Europeans. They would have fought for Serbia again and for Macedonia against Muslim Albanians, had they needed to fight.

There was no need for us to fight in 1999. We could easily have kept out of Serbia's small conflict. We could easily have kept out of conflicts all around the world since 1945.

We could have kept out of the conflicts in 1914 and in Europe from 1939 too. Nationalism with foresight would have averted the two world wars altogether, or kept us out of World War II in Europe. We have not learnt a thing.

There remain those in the West who blame war upon nationalism, but our rejection of nationalism since the two world wars has proven more militaristic than nationalism was. It has proven more violent.

Nationalism confines us to our wars and wars in our people's interests. Globalism has no limits in the wars that it starts or it joins.

Multiculturalism and other globalism draw us into other people's wars that our nationalism would have left alone. Globalism embarks upon wars all over the world without nationalistic regard for our soldiers suffering and dying.

Globalist wars can be for money. They can be for ideology, such as the so-called humanitarian wars for multiculturalism. They can be wars against any race on behalf of that race or another race, but never on behalf of our race.

Protecting white people would be racism. Leaving white people to die is multiculturalism.

For Other People's God and Country

Without nationalism or Christian faith, we still set off for war, but not for God and Country, at least not our God and Country. What had been our call for God and Country became our call for the multicultural globe, to which we expect each other to subscribe. We fight for other races, their gods, and countries.

Fixated with fighting white prejudice, it is hard to see what we support, except everybody else. Unlike our forebears, we fight each other over race and religion, while refusing to fight other races and religions. Instead of fighting other people's intolerance of us, we fight fellow white people's intolerance of others.

For the first time in Western history, we are sending our soldiers off to wars without conviction in God and often without Countries. Through past wars, our countries had Christian conviction to offer our servicemen and women, even if individuals among us did not. We stood with them as Countries, even if our leaders did not, before ideologies took hold of us.

Michael Weinstein, an American Jew, formed the Military Religious Freedom Foundation in 2005, but the freedom he espoused was not ours. He accused Christians in the American military, including chaplains, sharing their faith of treason and "spiritual rape" as serious as sexual assault. In 2013, the American military threatened court martial for soldiers proselyting any religion.

In our spirit of inclusion, we do not fight Muslims. We recruit them. While we forbid Christians from publicly preaching, we invite Muslim clerics to do so, even if they damn our dead when they do.

The West does not fear Muslims. We fear Christians.

Ancient Chinese general Sun Tzu's *The Art of War* commanded warriors to know their enemy. The West cannot know our enemies because we no longer know ourselves. We know only multiculturalism, so know nothing of race and culture: ours or anyone else's.

Having lost all sense of our cultural heritage, we cannot recognise other people's cultural heritage, which they defend and assert. We refuse to identify and confront Islam because we refuse to distinguish one culture from another, thus one religion from another.

Muslims treat fellow Muslims in Western armies as traitors, while we dare not wonder whether Western countries can fight wars in Muslim countries with Muslims among our soldiers. We do not want wars anyway, except against Christians.

Multiracial militaries are supposed to be less able to make war. Ours compromise our capacity for defence.

Instead of God and Country, we send our soldiers off to war with faith in multiculturalism: in other people's gods and countries. It is not very much.

If other races send their soldiers off to war without religious conviction, they at least send them with conviction in their countries and races. They are not dying for anybody else, while we send our men and women to die for everybody else.

September Eleven, 2001

None of the small applause we receive from other races lasts beyond the next time we do not accede to them. The West's acceptance of refugees and other immigrants from other races brings us no favour from those races. Neither does our provision of trillions of dollars in foreign aid and domestic welfare payments. Our support for Muslims at war brings us no favour from Muslims.

We do not expect their favour or applause. We do not think in such terms.

On Tuesday, the eleventh of September 2001, nineteen Muslim

Arabs, of whom many had lived and studied in America, simultaneously hijacked four domestic aircraft bound from America's east coast to her west coast. They had given no warning. They made no demands. The Arabs crashed two aeroplanes into the twin towers of the World Trade Centre, New York and a third aeroplane into the Pentagon military headquarters in Washington.

Hijacking aircraft laden with fuel for long flights maximised the destruction. Acting on a working Tuesday morning maximised the numbers of deaths.

The fourth aeroplane was headed to Washington to kill more people when the passengers, alerted by mobile telephone to the other suicide attacks, risked their lives already lost to overcome the hijackers. In the ensuing fracas, the aircraft crashed into a Pennsylvania field.

Three thousand people, including twenty-six hundred Americans, died that morning. Among the dead were hundreds of New York firefighters, who had entered the burning towers to help survivors escape before the towers collapsed. They perished heroes, trying to save people's lives, but an Australian broadcaster hating Americans so much abused the dead firefighters for arrogance.

Expert opinion quickly laid blame for the attacks on al-Qaeda. The Muslim terrorist organisation owed its origins to ferocious Muslim assaults upon Soviet troops in Afghanistan through the 1980s.

Most races on earth cast collective guilt upon other races and religions harming them, but not us, not since the Holocaust. We cast collective guilt upon us, collectively blaming ourselves. An America-hating Australian journalist blamed the September 2001 attacks on Western foreign policy towards Iraq, without any evidence to link that policy or Iraq to the attacks.

With our Western presumption that people are all one and the same and really quite reasonable, there came the suggestion that America should respond to the attacks by sitting down with al-Qaeda to understand Muslim grievances towards America. We had no thought of sitting down with Macedonians that year trying to understand Macedonian grievances towards Albanians.

For the most part, the 2001 attacks made America more popular than she had been for years. We love victims.

Instead of basking in our sympathy, America snapped awake

from her slumber, to a point. She aided rebels fighting the Muslim Taliban government in Kabul that abetted al-Qaeda. She prepared to attack al-Qaeda training camps in Afghanistan before more terrorists came.

White people who had wanted us to kill Serbs to protect Albanians did not want us killing Afghans to protect Americans. They insisted an Afghan's life was worth as much as an American's life, as only people without loyalties would. They had not said a Serb's life was worth as much as an Albanian's life.

With every military response, America's popularity waned. The more she dared to fight back, no longer the victim but the warrior, the more unpopular she became.

Conspiracy theorists blame Western, particularly American, governments for anything bad, rather than blame other races. As they would, they had already decided the Americans concocted the attacks. Like all good conspiracies, the less evidence it existed, then the bigger the conspiracy must be. This one must have been gargantuan.

War without Enemies

Conflicts in the Balkans and elsewhere had failed to awaken the West to the world returning to racial and cultural conflicts. The September 2001 attacks also failed to rouse us.

After the 2001 attacks, Americans rushed out to buy books about Islam, trying to understand why those nineteen Muslim hijackers wanted to kill them. Muslims did not buy books about America.

No Western leader associated the atrocities with race or religion, bar Italy's prime minister Silvio Berlusconi. "We should be confident of the superiority of our civilisation," he said a week afterwards, "which consists of a value system that has given people widespread prosperity and guarantees respect for human rights and religion. This respect certainly does not exist in Islamic countries."

Arab countries demanded that Berlusconi apologise. Western leaders distanced themselves from his comment. *Time* magazine called it a gaffe. Berlusconi said that he had been misunderstood.

The perpetrators of the attacks saw themselves as being at war with America, but America did not. After the attacks, American president George W Bush promptly attended a mosque in support of Muslims. Bush accused the terrorists of waging war against freedom.

The terrorists never said that. We did.

In response, the West waged our war not against Islam or Arabs, but against terror. It was much like our redefinition of World War II to have been against fascism and prejudice instead of Germany and our other wartime foe Japan.

Bush and the rest of the West's war on terror was a war without enemies, as was our subsequent talk of war against extremism. Our world and wars remain ideological, without trace of race, religion, or people.

In our ideological frame of mind, any evil in September 2001 was perpetrated not by Muslim Arabs but by human beings, without mention of race or religion. In time, it was as if the perpetrators had been characterless spirit beings.

In this conflict, there is envy and contempt, admiration and derision. There is not, from our side, discrimination.

Whatever the West is, we are not defending it. That is more than our right, as individuals. It is our expectation.

We do not defend Western countries and people because we do not countenance the collective identities upon which such a defence would be predicated. We do not group Muslim terrorists or their victims, even when we are the victims.

War is personal. We are not. There are no "we" and "they," only people, as far as the vanishing West is concerned.

Ours is a world without enemies. There are only people like us.

We call Islamic terror attacks on humanity, but the terrorists do not believe they are attacking humanity. They kill us, because they want to kill us. Until we acknowledge that we are the targets in this conflict, we will never escape it.

The War That Is Not

The day the towers fell, it seemed the world had changed. It did not change. People spoke of tall buildings never again being built, but they continued being built. Things hardly changed at all.

Classifying Muslim terror as something other than war does more to avoid war than everything else we have done. Ours is the war that is not; it never was. It is a non-war effort.

Like wars, we dispense with the truth, compromising the morality of peacetime to pursue our non-war effort. Within a very short time, we started referring to the September 2001 attacks not by the attackers but by the date on which they occurred: "nine/eleven," in the American way of numbering dates.

We stopped calling them attacks. They became a tragedy. They sounded accidental.

The West does not defend our countries, cultures, or races. We defend our ideologies. We defend multiculturalism.

Crime has not impinged upon our multicultural ideals. Neither will terror.

The West refuses to allow the conflict with Islam to be a clash between civilisations, because our ideologies of inclusion command there be only one civilisation, of which we are all equally part. No mere matter of civilisation is going to interrupt business.

Values cannot be in conflict, because we insist values are universal. Cultures cannot be in conflict, because we are abandoning ours. If we do not believe that we are already a unitary world, we think that we should be.

Ours are clashes without civilisation. We have only ideology and economics we remain doggedly determined to keep.

Islamic terror has only made us all the more determined to defend our multicultural dream. It has made us more desperate than ever to defend other races and their cultures from ours.

When a Muslim among our residents or citizenry kills us, we call that domestic, not Islamic, terror, as if we are just as much to blame. There are still deaths and destruction, but a different moniker.

If the mindsets of criminals do not perturb us from constructing them in our global image without race or religion, there is no reason the mindsets of terrorists should. They are more clients to rehabilitate.

Terrorism became too judgemental a concept. It is just another crime, and we have long stopped being fussed about crime. Instead of being terrorists, they are criminals, and everything is fine.

Only multiculturalism matters. Nothing deters us from defending diversity in what we insist is our multicultural wonderland.

We are determined not to let the terrorists win, by which we do not mean defending our races and cultures, saving white people's lives. We mean maintaining our hospitalities to other races and cultures. We think that to abrogate in any way the generosities we have discovered since the Second World War would mean that we lose. We are accommodating Islam as we have never before accommodated the beliefs of people attacking us.

It is an ideological victory in an ideological war: holding fast to the thoughts in our heads. We win by losing: losing our countries. We would lose by winning: saving our races. It is absurd, but it makes perfect sense to us.

The Religion of Peace

There are more than thirty-five thousand Koran verses, hadiths, Muslim scriptures, and other sharia commanding or encouraging violence, war, annihilation, corporal punishment, hatred, boycott, humiliation, or subjugation of others. They do so primarily against non-Muslims.

The intrinsically violent nature of Islam was common knowledge, before multiculturalism prohibited candour, honesty, and meaningful discourse about race or religion. While the rest of the world, including Muslims, can see the links, the West refuses to link race or Islam to terror any more than we link them to crime or anything else bad.

Islamic terror does not drive us to defend Christians but Muslims. Islam has no need to reform. The West insists it is already good.

Without regard for the Koran or the actions of Muslims, we insist that Islam is a religion of peace. The West, not Muslims, came up with that one.

We fob off Muslim terror with phrases such as "the majority of peace-loving Muslims." The only evidence that such a majority exists are the Muslim community leaders saying so and our new-found confidence in other races and cultures.

We do not treat the crimes of our past so particularly. No lamenting of Western history is tempered with reference to the majority of peace-loving Christians or peace-loving white people.

We link the Holocaust with our past prejudices, but refuse to link Muslim terror with Islam. Most Muslims going about their ordinary days might not be trying to kill anyone, but neither were most Germans before or during World War II. There was no defence for the majority of peace-loving Germans, let alone the majority of peace-loving Nazis. Most Nazis wanted neither war nor the genocide upon which Adolf Hitler embarked.

Muslim terrorists make no efforts to negotiate peace like Hitler's deputy Führer flying to Britain in 1941. We arrested Rudolf Hess and imprisoned him for the rest of his life. We stopped searching for peace with Germany in 1939 and Serbia in 1999, but keep insisting we are at peace with Muslims.

We excuse Muslim terrorists for being nice, but easily led. If we contemplated the same of Europeans, then we would see Nazi storm troopers as having been nice, but easily led.

The Koran calls upon Muslims to carry out jihad. Whether jihad means internal struggle, external violence, or both, it lacks peace and contentment.

Hitler's book *Mein Kampf* translates roughly as *My Struggle*, thus *My Jihad*. We do not treat his struggle as peaceful, but we are certain Islamic jihad is a peaceful pursuit.

So confident are we in the peaceful nature of Islam, we accuse Islamic terrorists of perverting or misusing Islam. We do not accuse Hitler of perverting or misusing Nazism, nationalism, or racism.

With our dogma of diversity, we insist that we know Allah's will better than Muslims know it. Evidence otherwise, we dismiss.

Jihadists became another euphemism we use to distinguish Muslim terrorists from other Muslims. Because we think all religions are equal and Islam bears no relation to terror, we also call Christian criminals jihadists, although they have no thought of jihad.

Losing their Religion

Muslims tell us they are killing us in the name of Islam. We do not believe them. Religion is not in play, not for the West, however much Muslims think it is.

Among the plethora of Muslim terrorist networks arose Islamic State, but even Islamic State we do not call Islamic. We call it Daesh. Only the headline changed.

We might refer to Islamic terror being religiously motivated, without mentioning the religion. We might describe female Muslim terrorists as wearing headscarves or veils, without mention of the religion associated with wearing headscarves or veils. We might refer to Muslim terrorists simply as zealots.

The West invented the idea of radical Islam, as against normal moderate Islam. Only radical Islam might harm us we insist, if hypothetically Islam could.

Muslims correct us, but we ignore their corrections. There is only Islam.

We distinguish Muslim extremists from other Muslims, although the only distinction is that extremists are terrorists. We do not distinguish racist extremists from other racists, or fascist extremists from other fascists.

More often than not, we call Muslim criminals and terrorists not real Muslims. We might call them Islamists, distinguishing them from Muslims. It would have been like referring to the Nazis killing Jews as Nazists, unlike other Nazis.

Every right we claim for ourselves, we grant terrorists, except one. We deny them their right to decide their religion. They think they are Muslims. We insist they are not. We reduce their religion to our definition.

Conversely, Muslims drinking alcohol and frequenting prostitutes without committing crimes or terror retain their right to choose their religion. They are Muslims, because they say they are.

Religious Conviction

The problems associated with Muslim immigration are essentially the same in nature as those associated with interracial immigration, although they are among the severest in scope. Of all the racial and cultural conflicts the West refuses to acknowledge, none are more striking than people's conflicts with Muslims.

Islam separates the world into *Dar al-Harb* (the countries of chaos) and *Dar al-Islam*. The West is chaos. Islam brings order.

In the years since 2001, Muslim terrorists have killed more than a thousand ordinary Europeans, North Americans, and Australasians in hotels, buses, railway stations, nightclubs, concerts, theatres, and elsewhere. They have killed many more people of other races around the world.

Islamic terror makes the failure of multiculturalism all the more obvious. It could have challenged the West's refusal since the Holocaust to confront, even consider, issues of race and religion, but we remain steadfast. It has not led the West to turn from ideology and confront reality. Nor has it inspired us to find again the nationalism that other races never lost.

The irreligious West does not understand religion. Western secularity cannot comprehend religious conviction.

Calling Islam fascist makes Islam political rather than religious; we understand politics. Islamic fascism is another Western construction separating Islam from militancy, categorising militant Islam with Nazism.

We call Islam an ideology because we understand ideologies, like communism, multiculturalism, and humanism, but religions are not ideologies. Ideologies have only human authority, weak as that is. Muslims believe they act with the authority of Allah, revealed in the Koran and other texts.

Mere ideologies do not motivate other races as they motivate us. Our only religious conviction is that all religions are equal: that Islam is irrelevant to crime, terror, and war. Thus there can be no Islamic crime, terror, or war, whatever Muslims happen to think.

Funding Islam

Much as we have spent decades blaming crime on economic disparities, we do the same for terror. We think ending poverty will defeat terrorism, in spite of so many terrorists around the West coming from wealthy, or at least financially comfortable, families.

Primarily in the Middle East, rich Muslims reward poor Muslims who kill Westerners and Jews. They reward the families of Muslims who die doing so, in capitalist-style reward and incentive dependent upon the killers' sense of family instead of individualism.

Muslims do not suffer because of Islamic crime and terror, not in the West. Instead, we reward them, without thought of what rich Muslims are doing.

The West particularly loves Muslims. We prefer Muslims to Christians.

We try to keep Muslims, especially young Muslim men, of whom there are many, from committing more crime and terror by funding their community and other groups, although it has not deterred them from crime and terror so far. Why the company of other Muslim men should discourage them from violence instead of encouraging them towards it is not obvious, but we have great confidence in the peaceful influence of Muslims.

We think playing sport will keep their minds from everything else. It plainly does not, although watching sport turns our minds from everything else.

Presuming that money can buy anything, we give Muslims money hoping that will dissuade them from crime and terror, although Western disability pensions do not keep them from travelling to the Middle East and joining Islamic militias. It pays their fares.

We might punish those soldiers by terminating their pensions, but we do not question the Western welfare systems and processes by which people able enough to be soldiers in the Middle East could be assessed to be disabled in the West. The systems and processes continue, rather than anyone missing out.

Causes of Terror

Islam differs between races because races differ. Muslim Malays differ from Muslim Arabs because Malays differ from Arabs.

The West works hard to find root causes of terror other than race or Islam, because we think redressing such causes will prevent further terror. The more we are attacked, the harder we try.

Education does not prevent terror. It educates terrorists.

Employment does deter terror. It creates more opportunities for terror.

Most meaninglessly of all, we blame generic workplace issues when a Muslim kills his colleagues. The killer does not. We presume that different races working together coalesce, but all working together seems to do is further convince those who would kill us they should.

We blame Islamic terror on social exclusion, but not by Muslims, by us. Yet, persecuted Christians and other religious minorities in Muslim and other countries, as well as the Falun

Gong in China, have not become terrorists.

Muslims are at least as violent in countries they dominate as they are in countries they do not. Muslim terror affects Muslim countries, too.

Unwilling to consider race or religion being relevant, we increasingly can conceive no other explanation for Muslims committing crime or terror than mental illness. The only evidence of that mental illness might be the crime or terror, but that is enough.

Our failure to distinguish religions maligns our own. Islamic clerics calling for our deaths become synonymous with Christian parish priests smiling at suburban church fêtes. If schools prohibit Muslim meetings because of security concerns, they will ban Christian meetings too.

The more menacing Muslims become, the more we wish we could end all religion. We start with our own.

Staving off Prejudice

While we refuse to discriminate, other races discriminate. So do other religions.

Kaffir is Arabic slang derogating non-Muslims. Muslims refuse to respect Western police for being Kaffirs.

When Muslim terrorists target white people, we ignore that. When they target non-Muslims generally, we ignore that. We blot from our minds not just Muslims killing and torturing, but them burning churches and forcibly converting others to Islam.

We are not worried about Muslim prejudices. We worry about ours.

Our enemy is white racism. We understand a need to defend ourselves from white people better than we see a need to defend ourselves from other races and their religions.

No number of Muslim terrorists, like no number of other terrorists and criminals, convinces us to worry about anything but white people's prejudice. We look for discrimination *against* Muslims, not *by* Muslims.

Wars often require all of a country's resources, but our primary response to Muslim terror has not been military. Nor has it involved the police. It has not involved curtailing immigration or winding back diversity and multiculturalism. Where our forebears spoke of eternal vigilance in terms of armed forces, we see it in terms of political will: to ensure people do not look less favourably upon Muslims.

Muslim terror makes us manage the Christians. We work hardest to answer not an enemy's terror, but the fears of our friends.

Rather than mentioning their race or religion, we identify terrorists by the scenes of their attacks, unless their birthplace or citizenship is Western. With the comfort of our convictions that immigrants are like the rest of us, joined with us in our mythical multicultural societies, we identify Western-born or Western-naturalised terrorists accordingly. If they were born in Britain or are British citizens, we call them British without concern that we malign our own, even if those terrorists would never describe themselves as British.

Meanwhile, we find and talk up victims of terror who are not white. We especially like Muslim victims.

We feel the world and our lives are most under threat not from other races or religions, but from the West slipping back into prejudice. We worry less about Muslim terror than about any backlash it might provoke among white people. We focus not on Muslims murdering white people, but upon white people subsequently being rude about Muslims.

We are better dead than rude. We only talk of religion to report the challenges Muslims supposedly face because of terror or to report the efforts of Muslims to prevent terror. In this fairy-tale world, Muslims are not perpetrators but victims and peacemakers.

We do not talk of Germans facing challenges since World War II. We do not mention Germans trying to avert war and holocaust beforehand.

People of other races retain their racial and religious loyalties, as the West no longer comprehends. When Muslims report fellow Muslims to Western authorities it is before terror attacks, to save those would-be assailants, not us, from harm. They are not so forthcoming with information *after* attacks.

Through it all, we are extraordinarily arrogant about white people's power and dismissive of other people's power to harm us, but we remember the Holocaust. It is arrogance that kicks us in our guts every day of our lives.

Wartime Propaganda

Allied propaganda during the Second World War encouraged us to fight Germans. Propaganda now encourages us *not* to fight Muslims.

In Western eyes, Islam's failings blemish all religion. Its successes are its alone.

We are determined to avoid any morsel of moral superiority above Muslims. Moral inferiority is fine.

While we believe that Europe's empires of old across the world were bad invasions, we insist that Moorish and Turkish invasions of Europe were good invasions. We appreciate the invaders' intervention, insisting they enriched us.

Subjugation and deaths are not so devastating when inflicted upon us. Other races agree.

The Moors occupied what became Spain and Portugal for almost eight hundred years. We now see the last Moor stronghold, Grenada, as a sort of multicultural nirvana before the intolerant Spaniards defeated the emirate in 1492. That might seem long ago, but 1492 was also the year that Christopher Columbus arrived in the Americas. White Americans now regard themselves as occupiers of other people's land. The Spaniards evicted the last Moors in 1616.

Turkish invasions of Europe reached the gates of Vienna in 1529 and 1683. Among the many countries occupied by the Turks was Bulgaria, which did not regain her independence until 1878. After five hundred years, the Balkan League evicted the last of the Turks from the Balkans in 1912.

The multiculturalist West is not so xenophobic. We would have hugged the Moors and Turks. We would have bombed the Spaniards and Balkan League.

No other race on earth speaks as fondly of being invaded as we now do, but foreigners have ceased entering the West by invasion. Increasingly since World War II, they have come through our open arms.

The messages are clear: we owe them. The more that they come, the more we believe they enrich us. We would all be better off if the West finally vanishes.

During Iraq's war with Iran during the 1980s, Iraqi film-makers broadcast stories from history of Arab victories against Persians.

We on the other hand, with our non-war against Muslims, trawl through history to find wrongful acts by Christians. Unable to find them, we concoct them.

Whatever stories we tell, the villains are not Muslims. They are Christians. We make Christians the threat.

We judge Muslims by their clothes, not their terror. Blotting from our minds Islamic teaching as we blot from our minds Christian teaching, the Islam we revere is poetic, artistic: a dreamy emotional lure for a West that understands only dreams and emotion.

Our multicultural vision is a world without religion, but where Islam is a revered culture without Allah: an atheistic, godless Islam, as only the ideological West could devise. No wonder Muslims kill us.

Abandoning Our Vulnerable

It has become fashionable to equate the division between Christianity and Islam with that between Protestantism and Roman Catholicism. Whatever else might be said of our past, we could walk along British streets without feeling alien or afraid.

The West equates Islamic terror with Irish Republican terror, but the latter did not claim to act in the name of God. It was Irish, not Roman Catholic, nationalism. Its objective was uniting All Ireland, not destroying England. Roman Catholic Englishmen and women did not kill their compatriots for Ireland.

We judged the Irish having regard to everything the Irish did. We do not judge Muslims at all.

For Muslims, we acknowledge the problems of multiculturalism that we do not acknowledge for ourselves. While we insist their religion is irrelevant to their being criminals or terrorists, we allow their religion to excuse them from criminal convictions and punishments that they would otherwise incur.

Nationalism protects people not as strong as the strongest. When the West turned against our racial and religious loyalties, we betrayed most of all our poor and vulnerable.

Police and community services allowed thousands of poor English girls to be abused by Muslim Asian men across the north of England rather than risk being accused of racism or religious prejudice. When police did not ignore the girls' plight, they prosecuted the girls, rather than irritate Muslims.

Social harmony requires us to appease immigrants, especially when they harm us. Muslims murdered some of the English girls.

Sure enough, when the police finally began investigating the assaults, the abusers accused the police of racism. Authorities concealed the race and religion of Muslim rapists from the English public, while police continued insisting that race and religion were irrelevant. Muslims admitted they targeted English girls because if they assaulted Muslim girls, they would be shot.

Morality being tribal, immigrant men raping and killing white women and girls are not being immoral in their eyes because their race remains unaffected. Muslims who condemn drug use while producing and distributing heroin are not being hypocritical, because they are not selling heroin to Muslims.

We are individuals: no longer tribal in any meaningful way; no longer moral. We aggressively accuse each other of racism and determinedly defend ourselves from accusations of racism, while white people suffer and die.

Coexistence

In the late 1970s, the Australian civil service warned the Australian government that Muslim immigrants would never integrate into Western societies. The Australian prime minister fobbed off those warnings.

Education makes our children whatever we want them to be. Thus we assume education can make other people's children whatever we want them to be, but parents of other races are not like us. They teach their children their heritage, as we no longer teach our children ours.

While we imagine new generations becoming like us, Western-born Muslims are more likely than older Muslims to believe the name of Islam warrants terror. Around the West, terrorists are increasingly locally born.

Muslim criminals and terrorists are often good family men. We are not their families.

When Muslim immigrants do seem to integrate in the West, they are vulnerable to their family members harming and even killing them for having abandoned their heritage. Those family members feel their honour and their family honour require it.

The West no longer comprehends honour. Being individuals, we do not really comprehend families.

When talk of racial and religious integration becomes too blatantly unbelievable, we espouse different races and religions living peacefully side by side. Mere coexistence is a weak vision for a place, but it is the vision that remains after we give up trying to create multicultural communities, without admitting that we gave up.

Even coexistence is more Western fantasy. Many Muslims believe that democracy violates Islam because only Allah can make laws.

Retaining their religious conviction, Muslims believe that coexistence between different religions denies the sovereignty of Allah. They are right. The Koran requires Muslims to convert non-believers.

By refusing any paramountcy for Christianity, multiculturalism also denies the sovereignty of God, but the West is uninterested in God. Western churches are uninterested in Christianity.

We imagine Muslims peacefully coexisting with other religions, but they cannot peacefully coexist with each other. Within Western countries, immigrants have no reason to confine their violence and threats of violence to their own, but will mete them out upon us when they want to. That is multiculturalism.

Islamophobia

The West has responded to recent Islamic terror with a new word and concept: Islamophobia, a fear or disliking of Muslims. Akin to any other ideological phobia that white people supposedly suffer, it can only be irrational.

We defend Muslims from discrimination because we defend everyone from white people's discrimination, but never was there a crueller, more oppressive word than so-called Islamophobia. It is imposed upon the only non-Muslims on earth welcoming Muslims: white people.

Refusing to consider issues of race or religion rationally, the West is certain that any white person considering those issues fears difference. The person fears diversity.

We love diversity so fervently. Not loving diversity seems irrational.

Among the thoughts and words forbidden for being Islamophobia is any rational consideration of the possible impact upon us or others of a growing Muslim population. We cannot so much as ponder the topic.

Refusing to defend our religion and rest of our cultures or to imagine anything undesirable about Muslims or Islam, we conclude that any resistance to Muslims asserting their religion over us must be irrational. Any hesitation to wrap our arms around Muslims, welcoming their mosques and minarets, makes us guilty of Islamophobia. Not enthusing for life under sharia would be Islamophobia.

The problem the West has with Islamophobia is that the word exists. It further shuts down rational consideration of Islam, multiculturalism, and sharia.

In place of Islamophobia, an honest term would be anti-Muslimism, akin to anti-Semitism, anti-communism, or anti anything else. It presumes neither rationality nor irrationality in a person's opposition to Muslim immigration, Islam, or sharia. It presumes neither fear nor a lack of fear.

Muslim-sceptic or Islam-sceptic would be simply questioning or even concern about growing Muslim populations and any future imposition of sharia. Questioning of anything is rational.

Freedom of speech cuts all ways. Freedom to support Muslim immigration, sharia, and Islam ought to be freedom to express concern about or to oppose Muslim immigration, sharia, and Islam. Free discussion about the grounds of that concern or opposition allows people to decide rationally whether those grounds are rational or irrational: whether that concern or opposition is rational or irrational.

The only real Islamophobia is the West's irrational fear of rationally examining Islam. We accept Islamic crime and terror, while being furious at white people concerned for our families, races, countries, and cultures.

Never are our Western ideologies of inclusion and equality more manifestly incoherent, illogical, and self-defeating than they are when feminists and homosexuals protest Islamophobia. Logically, they should be at the forefront of opposing Muslim immigration, but ideologies of inclusion and equality are not predicated upon logic.

Concerned only about white people, Muslim men can beat women but still Western feminists welcome them. Muslims can beat, imprison, and kill homosexuals, but still Western homosexuals welcome them.

In spite of the West refusing to believe that anything is innate, there is a view that women are naturally submissive and men naturally assertive. While white women have become increasingly estranged from white men and white men have become increasingly emasculated since 1945, no men have become more assertive than Muslim men.

Homosexuals might be similarly submissive. They can seem very feminine.

We refuse to link crime, terror, and other wrongdoing with Islam. Instead, we link them with Islamophobia. We blame us.

However poorly some Muslims treat each other, their greater detachment is with non-Muslims. With our incapacity to imagine racial or religious differences, any greater crime rates among Muslims than people of other religions are not reasons for us to fear Muslims. We treat them as evidence of our supposed discrimination.

We would rather be dead than be wrong. Faced with a choice between fighting for life and lying down to die, ours is a soulless surrender to fate.

If we saw a white woman move from her seat on a train because a swarthy-faced man wearing a backpack sat down beside her, we would watch her with contempt. We might even venture forth a self-satisfied smile that we stayed behind, before his backpack blasts us both to our free-willing deaths.

Hate Crimes

When people hate, they harm only themselves, provided they do not hit, rape, or kill others. The emotion grinds away from within.

Conversely, when people hit, rape, or kill, they harm other people. Whether they happen to hate those other people is immaterial.

We respond to Muslim terror with constraints not upon

Muslims, but upon white people. We are more concerned with other races' feelings than with white people's safety.

In particular, there are the infamous hate crimes. Hate crimes are like hate speech. Only white people are guilty.

Designating a crime a hate crime can simply increase the criminal's punishment. We are the only race on earth to consider crimes committed against people of other races to be worse than crimes committed against people of our race. In this Age of Ideology, the reasons someone slits a person's throat matter more than our frail throat being slit.

Hate speech becomes a hate crime when the government, police, or another human authority steps in. White people unfazed about robbery, rape, and murder become fiery advocates for law and order when someone from another race or religion feels upset, or they fear might feel upset.

Most crimes depend upon the criminal's criminal intent, but not hate crimes. Hate crimes depend upon other people's perception, however innocent the perpetrator's mind.

In Britain, hate crimes include words or actions perceived by the victim or any other person to be motivated by hostility or prejudice based on a person's race or perceived race or a person's religion or perceived religion. The words or action does not have to be hostile, but merely perceived as being hostile in the mind of another person.

So obsessed are we with protecting other races and their religions, we empower them. Discrimination, vilification, and hate speech increasingly mean whatever protected groups feel they should mean.

We make only some perceived prejudice illegal. Hating rich people is fine.

Hating the race or religion of the people who murdered your daughter is not. We have lost our freedom to feel.

In this Age of Ideology, a hate crime need not otherwise be a crime, or even otherwise be illegal. No one needs to be hurt, nor property damaged.

Taunting, mocking, or even simply disagreeing with Muslims can all be hate crimes. We shut down any challenge, questioning, or resistance to Islam.

Along with immigrant privilege, the West grants specific Muslim privilege. Never before has victimhood been so easy.

Muslims as Jews

World war and holocaust we denote Western crimes. Muslim crime and terror pale by comparison, we think, as Jews in Treblinka would have thought.

Responding to Jews as a race, Adolf Hitler had no regard for religion, but we think of Jews by their religion. We thus construe Hitler's treatment of Jews as being as much about religion as race.

Hitler made negative generalisations about Jews. We are not going to raise even the smallest spectre of negative racial or religious generalisations being true, for fear of where Hitler's generalisations led.

We refuse to link race or religion to crime and terror, because that is what Nazis did. Instead, we link religion to measures protecting us from terror, because they fall disproportionately upon Muslims. That makes Muslims not terrorists, but victims of terror.

We protest security measures protecting us. Muslims protest security measures obstructing them, or simply hearing and watching them.

We do not discriminate between religions, or between one religious prejudice and another. We thus equate Islamophobia to anti-Semitism. Muslims do not.

In our minds, Muslims are the Jews of our time. We lump them together as victims of white people's prejudice.

The Holocaust remains the most profound incident of racial and religious profiling in Western history, never to be repeated. To be wary of Muslims might legitimise Hitler's wariness of Jews, we worry. We are only wary of white people.

Having opened our borders to all, we cannot close them to Muslims but not others. Reinstating discrimination against particular races or religions would smack of the Nazis zeroing in upon Jews.

Considering the possibility that discrimination against Muslims is reasonable would be like considering the possibility that anti-Semitism was reasonable, we fear, which would be to consider the possibility the Holocaust was reasonable. Other races and religions harming us do not justify us discriminating against them any more than Nazi fears of Jews harming Germany could justify the Holocaust.

If religious pluralism fails, then multiculturalism fails, as happened with Jews in Europe. We persevere with Muslims because Germany gave up with Jews, without contemplating any distinctions between religions. There was no more profound expression of the failure of multiculturalism than the Holocaust.

Our dogged opposition to religious discrimination means we are unwilling to deal with threats grounded in religion, without punishing others. When the threats posed by Muslims finally require action, we take action against non-Muslims too, because they are not Muslim.

To prove we are not prejudiced, our war against terror is an equal opportunity war. Had the Second World War been fought on the same basis, we would have bombed Cornwall each time we bombed Germany.

Freedom from Speech

The West lauds our right to satirise religion, but our right to laugh is to laugh at our religion, not anyone else's religion. We have Jesus and Christians to mock.

Freedom of speech has become selective. The voices we want to hear are not those of white people.

Immigrant rights include freedom *from* speech: from hearing speech they dislike. Freedom *of* speech is theirs alone.

We become upset whenever white people criticise other cultures. We become upset when animals are maltreated. The two sensitivities conflict wherever other cultures mistreat animals.

Our rejection of prejudice normally prevails. Not much can silence Western animal rights activists, but Islamic and Jewish rules for the slaughter of animals silence them.

We are more worried about immigrants feeling upset than white people feeling upset. For white people, we demand tolerance.

When émigrés to the West offend Islam, we cop culpability too. The onus is upon us to censor anything offensive to Muslims.

When their offence leads to violent protests by Muslims, we do not question multiculturalism. We become more confident in the strength and maturity of multiculturalism because Muslim community leaders condemn their violence, while the violence continues.

The more that Muslims kill us, the more we fear them feeling offended. We become forever more determined not to offend them.

Not as brave as our forebears, our talk of tolerance for Muslims belies the fact that we are frightened to refuse them. The sword gets its reward.

We are not really as frightened of white people as we say that we are. We torment our own knowing that white people will not kill us in reply.

The West's approach throughout our multicultural experiment has been to ignore the bad and find something good we think comes of immigration. That usually means restaurants. Dismissing the sacrifices our forebears suffered in war and the lives of our compatriots and descendants, we enthuse for rapidly growing Muslim populations because at some point in our lives, we might want a kebab.

Muslim Nationalism

Only Islam and Christianity through history have made much of a religious nationalism crossing racial lines, albeit subordinate to race and to racism. The West no longer subscribes to racism or nationalism, but other races still do.

Immigrants to the West do not give up their identities, simply because we gave up our identities. They have not bought into Western individualism. Instead, they continue to identify with those of their race all over the world.

Muslims also identify with fellow Muslims all over the world. There is no Muslim individualism.

Religious nationalism is predicated not upon personal belief, but upon collective identity. Ignorance of the detail of their religion does not mean people lack conviction. Dedication to their religion does not depend upon people being devout.

We respect Muslim nationalism identifying with fellow Muslims as victims. Muslims attack people in one country for what they feel that other people of that race in other countries do to Muslims. We are often those people.

Muslims are not just defending each other. They are advancing each other.

We refuse to identify Muslims with fellow Muslims doing

wrong, but they continue to do so. War and terror strengthen Muslims' sense of Muslim identity, while further reducing the West's willingness to identify anyone as anything.

Muslims living in some Western cities reputedly danced in the streets to celebrate the September 2001 attacks on America. Western media reported only Muslim community leaders publicly condemning the attacks.

When we think about Islam, we place great credence in what Muslim community leaders tell us Islam expects of Muslims. It matters more than what Muslims believe Islam expects of them, or what Muslims actually do. Renegade imams who yell their anger at us so loudly and often they cannot help but occasionally be reported are dismissed as recalcitrant individuals.

We insist that Muslims condemning crime and terror represent all Muslims, believing their words are the norm among Muslims. They are not. It is good public relations. We understand public relations.

Unaware of the ploys behind public relations, many Muslims feel betrayed to hear what they feel is their community leaders capitulating to the edicts of multiculturalism: capitulating to the West. We could say the same of Western leaders betraying us to other races for multiculturalism, but defending us would be our nationalism.

Islamic Altruism

No terrorists' rant or rationale is in abstract, as our talk of wars against prejudice and terror are in abstract. They might hate liberty and democracy, fashion and music, but do not need to kill us because we like them.

Our blindness to race and cultural differences leaves us unprepared for a world that sees race and cultural differences. We who have abandoned our collective identities are ill prepared to fight people who have retained their collective identities. Our disloyalties leave us unable to deal with people of loyalty.

Unlike crime, terror is motivated by altruism. The amoral, individualist West does not understand altruism.

Muslims might fight because they feel insecure. They defend their religion and rest of their cultures as we individuals cannot imagine defending our religion and cultures, much as Muslims defended their religion and rest of their cultures in Afghanistan from another globalist ideology: communism. Theirs are senses of god, peoples, and civilisations akin to those leading our forebears to die on our behalf.

We abandoned our forebears. Other races have not abandoned their forebears.

Muslims might hate us, but do not need to hate us to value their races and cultures. Muslims are fighting us not in spite of multiculturalism, but because of it.

If Muslims are not fighting multiculturalism, they are fighting the end of religion it entails. Our Western world vision raises the spectre of there being no Arab, Persian, or other civilisations, much as it obliterates Western Civilisation.

Conversely, Muslims might fight us because they seek to conquer us. Most races seek conquest, of some form or another.

Muslims might dream of an Islamic caliphate. We think of the world as a multicultural caliphate.

Counterterrorism measures disproportionately affecting Muslims lead Muslims to accuse Western police of persecuting them. Police operations apprehending Muslim terrorists become unjust, motivating fellow Muslims to step into defend them, becoming terrorists too. Muslim terror never ends.

The multiculturalist West cannot comprehend anything but tolerance for crime and terror from other races and their religions, certain that it will save us from further attack. It has not saved us yet.

Solidarity with Muslims

While respecting talk of the Muslim world, we do not imagine there being a Christian world, not anymore. We *have* bought into the Western idea of individualism.

If we were to identify with fellow Christians or white people attacked by Muslims in other countries or even in our country, as Muslims identify with fellow Muslims, we would be called Islamophobic. We maintain our individualism when white people suffer isolation and despair, injury and death, refusing to defend our race or religion. Our dead do not matter.

We do not defend our brothers and sisters. We defend other people's brothers and sisters. We defend Muslims from accusations of terrorism, unable to believe Muslims could be terrorists.

When people of other races kill white people, our solidarity is not with our race. It is with those other races and their religions. Nobody is killing them, but we fear them suffering white people's racism.

Ours is selective solidarity, no less than nationalism. Instead of embracing the nationalism that other races retain, we embrace other races and their religions. We think they need common defence from us, as Jews needed defence from the Nazis through the Holocaust.

We care everything for what happens to everyone else, even if all they feel is offence. There is nothing white women like more than donning hijabs in solidarity with Muslim women against white men.

White women feel no such solidarity with Muslim women against Muslim men. That would be bigotry.

White women don hijabs. White men fast through Ramadan. Both declare their actions to the world. They might talk of solidarity with Muslims or inclusion, but it is submission, by a race that considers the faintest hint of maintaining its customs to be culturally insensitive to other races but considers the sorriest of submission to other races to be virtuous.

When someone attacks a Muslim, all Muslims feel attacked. That is nationalism.

That attack on a Muslim also makes white people feel attacked. That is multiculturalism.

When someone attacks a white person, that white person is alone. Nobody else cares. That is individualism.

Joining Islam

"Islam is the second religion, the second community in France," declared Abdelaziz Boumediene, President of the Movement for International Solidarity, in 2020. "Those who do not like us have only to leave France. France, we love it with its Muslim community or we leave it."

Nobody said the same of Christianity in France in 2020,

although Islam was still only the second religion. Boumediene was Muslim.

Other races have not bought into Western individualism. Neither really have we.

White people convert to Islam for the sense of belonging: the nationalism, strong family ethic, and self-belief that the West has forsaken. Like others adopting foreign religions, they are often lost, as Muslims from other races born Muslim are not. Western revolutionaries fighting their countries, race, and selves often care no more what the Koran says about anything than twentieth-century communists cared what *Das Kapital* had to say.

Two generations after the Second World War, our young men still set off to war. Now, they fight against us.

Through foreign eyes, white people remain Christian for being white, whatever we think. We only presume that white people remain Christian if they are bad.

White people who reject loyalty to their compatriots for being nationalistic find patriotic fervour to defend white people converting to Islam and committing terror against us. If we call them Muslim converts, it is to make them not really Muslim.

Those terrorists might adopt Islamic names, but we continue describing them by their Christian names. Only good Christians can renounce their religion: their Christian identity.

Terrorist Rights

Our preoccupation with rights reached its logical conclusion with Islamic terror. Muslim terrorists are individuals with individual rights, because we insist everybody is an individual with individual rights. Denying terrorists their rights would make them the victims.

As only ideology could do, we equate terrorists' civil liberties with our liberties. Our persisting fear of fascism leaves us suspicious not of people from other races and religions but of Western police and security forces. We are more fearful of white people's powers and uniforms than we fear the people from whom they are trying to protect us.

Only the West separates justice from people, our people. Bathing other races in rights so they can use those rights against us, they do.

If we had fought World War II the way we fight Muslim terror, then we would have paid Germany compensation for any humiliation due to the Dunkirk evacuation. Germany could have petitioned the High Court of Justice in London for an injunction against the Normandy landings.

Western laws no longer defend the West. They defend people at war with the West.

We do not detain members of terrorist organisations committing acts of violence for lengthy periods without charge. We refuse to return them to countries that do.

Whatever the risk to Western lives, we do not subject foreign terrorists to foreign jurisdictions treating them more harshly than we would. Terrorism qualifies them for refugee status.

Western lawyers champion Muslims' rights, indifferent to Western lives. So do Muslim lawyers.

So little do we value each other and ourselves beneath our cavalcade of rights, we stand nobly estranged from the consequences. Giving everyone the full gamut of rights, uninterested in who benefits and who suffers, our introspective ideologies blind us to blood.

Rights matter more than relationship. We are not deterred from helping people of other races because they might maim the woman and her baby at the end of our street. We do not countenance discrimination even to save our brother from being assaulted or our daughter from being raped. If a terrorist's life is worth no less than our compatriots' lives, then it is worth no less than our children's lives. If we knew the victim would be us, we still would not discriminate.

We are so different to other races, for whom defending people who threaten or killed scores of their race would be immoral. We think all lives are equal, including our own. We divorce from our thinking our people who die.

Anything else would be nationalism. Anything else would be racism.

Without nationalism, Western humanitarianism helps people who kill us. Not even to save ourselves have we the mood to deny the rest of the world.

If anything, endangering our lives makes us proud. We sacrifice white lives on humanitarian grounds.

Bad Christians

The West refuses to fear other races and cultures. We only fear white people and cultures.

Multiculturalist ideology deems any concern about a race or religion to be irrational, except white people and Christianity. Public railing against America, Europe, or the entire West does not make Muslims guilty of Ameriphobia, Europophobia, or Westophobia. Those words do not exist. There is no Christophobia because, since the Holocaust, we think fearing or disliking Christians is perfectly rational, even sensible.

Islamophobia and anti-Semitism include prejudice, no matter how minor, against Muslims by their religion and Jews by reason of their race or religion. They also include any rational consideration of Muslim and Jewish influence upon the West.

There is no corresponding word for prejudice, no matter how rabid, against white people or Christians. Irrational criticism of Christian influence on the West flows unchallenged.

We believe Jews and anyone else telling us that Christianity fosters violence as we will not believe that other religions or the opponents of religion foster violence. It is the perspective that blames Christian Europe for the Holocaust.

News services refuse to report criminals and terrorists targeting Christians. In reporting crime and terror, religion is relevant not when a victim is Christian, but when a criminal or terrorist is, however much it might promote prejudice against Christians. The exoneration of bad Muslims from being real Muslims is not one we extend to bad Christians.

When the wrongdoer is not white, his or her race remains irrelevant. Anything else might encourage racial prejudice.

Child abuse does not taint teachers, politicians, or any other perpetrators' professions as it taints Christian clergymen. Clergymen are treated as accomplices and conspirators for failing to understand the torment the abuse caused, at a time that only the victims understood. Naïvety is no excuse for Christians, as it is for criminals of other religions or of no religion.

While insisting that Muslim criminals and terrorists are individuals, we impose upon white people collective culpabilities for crime and terror. We have no trouble linking white people's racism, nationalism, or political opinion to crime and terror, even where there is no link in fact. We persecute, if not prosecute, people protecting us.

With commentary unthinkable about other races and without evidence that any of them are planning violence, America labels as potential terrorists white people concerned about illegal immigration, abortion, firearms control, and the expansion of federal powers. There is no caveat for the majority of peace-loving white people concerned about such issues.

In spite of the tens of millions of military veterans committing no crimes, war veterans are particular targets for American government concern because of terror unleashed by one veteran in Oklahoma City in 1995. Timothy McVeigh was agnostic, although we do not worry about agnostics. He was a child of divorced parents, but we do not link parental divorce to behavioural issues.

McVeigh thought he was avenging the American government's role in the 1993 deaths of seventy-six Branch Davidian cult members, including children, in Waco, Texas, but we do not trouble ourselves with motives excusing white people's crimes and terror. We only search for motives excusing crime and terror by other races.

We have a palpable enthusiasm for believing white people to be terrorists. It not only helps us disregard Islamic terror. It affirms our confidence that white people are the obstacles to multicultural harmony.

Government warnings about possible terror attacks are most telling. While insisting that we not consider race in speculating whether a person is a terrorist, the authorities only imagine that white people could be terrorists. In this fantasy world, patriots warning the police about terrorist attacks are black, Asian, or Arab.

So when police and other emergency services prepare their responses to terror, they are not supposed to consider potential terrorists being Muslim. Instead, they are supposed to imagine white terrorists. It leaves us unprepared for reality, but the vanishing West is already disengaged from reality.

Love and Terror

In 2011, another white terrorist murdered seventy-seven people, almost all of them his fellow Norwegians. It was a counter-attack in a war that white people are waging with each other, and had been waging for a while.

The killings were notable for a terrorist's race and religion being newsworthy, as it was not with Muslim terror, and for the extensive coverage of victims. Instead of disappearing as Muslim names did, his Norwegian name Anders Breivik remained at the fore.

There were no disclaimers that he was not a real Christian, although he had no Christian faith. He was called a cultural Christian, because he was Norwegian and identified with Christianity. White people are deemed to be Christians when they commit terror, as we are otherwise not.

No terrorist has been called a cultural Muslim. The West calls few, if any, terrorists Muslim at all.

The killings could have been a reason for Norwegians to start discussing interracial immigration. Instead, it was another reason not to discuss it. Norway continued welcoming immigrants.

Also welcoming immigrants was New Zealand. In 2019, an Australian killed fifty-one Muslims at two mosques in Christchurch.

Without apparent thought of Christianity, Brenton Tarrant objected to immigrants replacing white people across the West. In 2017 and 2018, he had become fixated with Islamic terror, presumably including the Bali bombings in 2002 in which eighty-eight Australians died among two hundred and two people dead.

After the Christchurch killings, the New Zealand prime minister promptly donned a hijab. A week after the killings, she joined twenty thousand people attending Muslim prayers in Hagley Park, Christchurch. Muslim calls to prayer were broadcast on radio and television throughout New Zealand.

We did not talk of Breivik and Tarrant feeling lost as we talk of Muslim terrorists feeling lost. There were no calls to integrate white people as there are to integrate Muslims.

Nobody suggested that we should sit down with white terrorists as we suggest of Muslim terrorists. There were no pleas to understand their motivations as we try to understand Muslim motivations, no calls to comprehend. Nor was there talk of how horribly we treated white people, as Muslim terror inspired talk about how horribly we supposedly treat Muslims. Instead of alleviating white terrorists' grievances as we try to alleviate Muslim terrorists' grievances, we scorned them.

We hated the white terrorists with vengeance we refuse to feel towards Muslim terrorists. We called them mad and evil.

Breivik's parents divorced when he was a year old. His mother raised him, hitting him, and telling him she wished he was dead.

Tarrant's parents also separated when he was young. His mother entered a relationship with a man who abused her and her children. His father killed himself in 2010.

The West assumes terrorists kill from hate, because we understand hate. We hate racism and religious prejudice.

There is no hatred levelled at people for their race or religion as fierce as that which we level at our fellow white people loyal to our race and religion, wanting to keep our countries. We laud other races with all glories, but spit to death anyone among us who breathes a few glories of our own. We damn and despise any self-respecting racism that bravely bares itself among us.

What we do not understand is love. Facing the necessity of war, our forebears across Europe and her colonies sent men like Breivik and Tarrant to fight and die. They fought to save us when necessity demanded that they harm the people who threatened us, without the hatred that we mete out today. If there was feeling in our forebears fighting their wars, it was love for our races, cultures, and countries. It was love for us, then unborn.

We do not understand devotion: people valuing a greater good enough to fight and to die. We just die. We talk of the world but value little more than our individual selves, and even that, not very much.

McVeigh, Breivik, and Tarrant survived the attacks they carried out. The sample is very, very small, but Western terrorists are not as willing to die as Muslim terrorists are.

Like the altruistic Muslims, Breivik and Tarrant loved and valued their culture and race. The 2011 and 2019 killings were remarkable not because they occurred, but because they had not occurred sooner and more often.

The Peace of Individuals

Our forebears across Europe, the Americas, and Australasia loved peace. In pursuit of peace, necessity sometimes demanded they fight, kill, and die in defence of our nations, race, and civilisation.

We have not simply lost the sense that our forebears fought and died for peace. We have rejected the idea that anyone could.

Our forebears equated justice, freedom, and security with defending our nations, cultures, and race. We equate them with losing ours.

Theirs was a nationalist pacifism. Ours is an individualist pacifism.

The necessity to defend peace remains, but ours is not the peace that our forebears craved. The peace we crave is not peace for millennia, but peace for the moment.

We have become lone individuals, fearing that relationships might draw us to battle. We do not fight, kill, or die for anyone else. We do not do anything for anyone else.

The wars that our forebears fought for peace, we no longer fight. Globalism is our overarching desperation to avoid conflict, however much people suffer. Multiculturalists, citizens of the world, leave people to die.

Rather than the freedom a country can be, freedom is ours alone, tucked in our tiny homes in our shrinking neighbourhoods. We have become careful where we walk by day and even more wary by night, without questioning our confinement.

We lock our doors and hide. It is our peace of mind, in the hollows of our heads: the peace of solitary individuals. Our pacifism is so terrified of war that we dare not step outside, but proudly we demand our compatriots not fight on our behalf.

Ours is the peace that American president John Kennedy rejected in his State of the Union address in 1963. "The mere absence of war is not peace."

We could have kept our countries without malice on our part, learning not to fight each other, but we are losing our countries without learning anything. We head straight to defeat.

Our forebears were never willing to surrender as much as we sacrifice for the sake of our ideals. No other race is willing now.

The Peace of Nations

In our determination to defend multiculturalism, we will see greater risks of terror in almost anything but Islam. That includes, in spite of all the evidence, racial homogeneity. Racially homogenous Japan has enjoyed more peace than we have known since 1945, but we imagine that diversity will sometime bring peace.

Multiculturalism was supposed to make our countries blueprints for a world without war, but relaxing our borders created conflict. People naturally congregate by race and religion, but multiculturalism forces races and religions together and thus into conflict. We cannot leave each other alone when we share the same cities.

Our forebears risked their lives in wars, but could generally come home to peace. Our soldiers can no longer walk Western streets safely. We have brought wars from our borders and beyond into our cities and streets.

A place in which people kill freely is not a country. Without nations, we are intrinsically insecure.

Other races have not made the same presumptions and pledges that we have. Suffering wars and massacres in the past makes them treasure their nations more. Race and nation remain matters of life and death: their own.

While the West pursues a world without borders, other races keep putting borders up. Some solution to the Sudanese Civil War was separating Sudan into two countries in 2011, partitioning the Muslim Arab north from the African, partially Christian, south. They all felt safer in separate countries.

Diversity was not their greatest strength in Sudan. Partition was. If the West is going to find peace again, then we will need to do the same.

National governments are safer not because governments are safer, but because nations are safer. Nationalism saves people lives.

If the West wanted peace between peoples, we too would want races safe with their religions within nations, but we do not want peace. We want multiculturalism.

For us to find security again, we have to love peace more than we hate war. We need to feel part of a people with race and religion; everyone else does. We need to believe in countries, distinct from one other, allowing self-determination not just for other races but also for ours. Peace requires peoples determining their destinies behind borders: the peace of nations.

There can be no peace without security. There can be no security without borders. National borders are in people's best interests.

Like neighbours, we need fences not to fight. If we are not willing to defend ourselves, we are willing to be destroyed.

Islamic Land

Equality is Western ideology. Other races and their religions discriminate.

Sharia includes the concept of dhimmi, by which Muslim countries allow non-believers limited rights of residence in return for paying punitive rates of taxation. Christians and Jews paid those additional taxes while Spain was under the control of the Umayyad Caliphate. Ordinary taxes went to programmes for Muslim welfare.

Israel, the Jews' ancient home, was the destination of several waves of Jewish immigration from Europe and elsewhere over centuries before and after the modern state of Israel was founded in 1948. Nevertheless, Arabs decided through the twentieth century that the whole Middle East is intrinsically Arab.

Arab countries making peace with Israel recognised that Israel was not Arab, but they did not make their lands any less Arab. They recognised the peace of nations.

Much of what is now Islamic land used to be Christian land. That includes Lebanon, where a Christian president in 1982 coined the term dhimmitude to describe Muslims becoming the majority and subordinating Christian and other minorities.

In spite of the persecution suffered by Christians in Islamic and other countries, the West's rejection of religious difference refuses to find common ground with Christians of other races, much as we refuse to find common ground with people of our race. Caring about Christians would be Christian nationalism. Protecting Christian minorities would be culturally insensitive to Muslim majorities.

Through the twentieth century, Christians fell from being twenty percent of the Middle Eastern population to five percent. Religious cleansing means Christianity faces extinction in the Middle East at the hands of the Arabs.

The multiculturalist West is uninterested. We pour huge payments of foreign aid to countries like Egypt and Pakistan, where particularly violent persecutions of Christians remain largely unchecked.

Coptic Christians have been in Egypt since before Mohammed was born, but Muslims regard Egypt as Islamic land. Violence against Copts has reduced the proportion of Christians from twenty percent of Egypt's population in the middle of the twentieth century to ten percent early in the twenty-first century.

We take none of the actions to protect Christians in Muslim countries that we took to protect Muslims in Christian Serbia and Macedonia in 1999 and 2001. We simply give victims refuge as we give everyone refuge, assisting the Christian Exodus.

There is no immigration to Muslim countries like Muslim and other immigration to the West. There is only emigration.

Not only Christians suffer in religious conflicts around the world. A Bangladeshi prime minister responded to the continuing massacres of Hindus and Buddhists in Bangladesh by saying that if Hindus and Buddhists wanted to live safely, they should either convert to Islam or go to India. Bangladesh is Muslim land.

Religious Replacement

The land the West does not respect is our own. The concept of Christian land we have rejected since the Holocaust, although we understand the problem that Christians can be.

The West has abandoned manufacturing, but we have no end of tribunals, commissions, and courts by which other races can vent their offence at even the meekest of criticisms. Theirs might be a brittle self-certainty, but it is self-certainty nevertheless: opportunism with the rights and money that we make available.

Whether it is crime, terror, living from welfare instead of seeking a job, or anything else, we treat other races only as victims of white people and our supposed prejudice. We do not treat them as anything ill. We do not regard them as beneficiaries of our largesse.

While we welcome immigrants no matter what they think of us and our cultures, they are not so tolerant of us. Muslims call us infidels and, nowadays, they are right.

We avert religious tensions by abandoning our religion. Other races do not.

Islam requires Muslims to pray, but does not specify the times or places to pray. When Muslims block Western streets, squares, and footpaths to pull out their prayer mats and kneel upon them in prayer, or when they demand rights to pray to Allah at work, they are asserting themselves and their cultures. They do not block cars and pedestrians in their countries.

We accede, waiting for them to finish their prayers or detouring around them in fear of being accused of bigotry if we complain. Leaving Islam unfettered, while removing from sight every vestige of our culture in fear of immigrants complaining, we call multiculturalism.

France fetters, a little. Her state secular atheism restricts all religions.

In 2004, France banned visible religious symbols from government schools. Nobody cared about banning Christian Crosses, but Muslims violently demanded that their girls wear headscarves. They were not demanding French people's rights to wear Christian Crosses.

Anti-Semitism

Schools, institutes, associations, and the like may well be geographically within Western countries, but we respect them being of other countries and races. We do not mind their prejudice against the West and Christianity any more than we mind such prejudice among white people. We agree with it.

The prejudice we oppose is against other races and religions. We object when Saudi schools in Britain teach anti-Semitism.

Muslim terrorists often target synagogues. They target Jews.

Anti-Semitism is rising in Western countries, but to blame Muslims for it would be Islamophobic. Unwilling to link prejudice with anyone but us, we focus upon our dwindling peoples, even if we know of no anti-Semitic white people.

Most Jews, at least those whose views reach the public space, remain more frightened of white people and any revival of our racism and nationalism than they fear Muslims. So do we.

Even in the rare instant when a white person acknowledges Muslim anti-Semitism, we blame white people. Blaming all prejudice on white people and presuming Muslims are among our many victims, we presume that our supposed prejudice against Muslims drives Muslims towards prejudice against Jews.

That Islam has been anti-Semitic since its inception and Islamic texts vilify Jews do not dissuade us. Neither does Muslims outside the West being no less anti-Semitic than Muslims living in Western countries; we imagine a world without countries anyway. Those matters simply affirm how extensive, pervasive, and influential we presume white people's prejudice to be and to have always been.

We fret only about white people's prejudice because we do not imagine anyone but white people carrying a Holocaust into effect. That presumption is Western arrogance. It is no less arrogant to think that we can cleanse Muslims of their anti-Semitism the same way that we have been rid of ours.

Most Jews make the same presumption. Some Jews do not.

Like other immigrants, the Jews who give up on multiculturalism and other anti-Western ideologies are those who realise that their greatest threats are not white people. For Jews, their greatest threats are Muslims.

Multiculturalism is achieving what Nazism failed to do: driving the Jews from Europe. Jews who worked hard to prevent the West committing another Holocaust are facing the first sense of a Holocaust from Muslims, but we and most Jews are not paying attention, as if Jewry died in the death camps and cannot die again.

Sharia

We do not normally compile or report data suggesting the size of modern-day Muslim populations in the West for fear of stoking white people's prejudice, except in some other context. Schooling is one other context.

Arguing the need for the West to recognise sharia is another, but when Muslims, if only with words and stickers, declare their sharia zones in English cities, we fob those declarations away. While we debate recognition of sharia, Muslims already enforce it.

We understand Jews wanting to live by their religion and other culture. We understand Sikhs, Buddhists, and other immigrants wanting to live by theirs. It is reasonable for Muslims to want to live by sharia.

For the West to imagine Muslims without sharia is fanciful. What do they do? Believe in Allah and his one true prophet Mohammed but disregard his teachings that he requires them to impose, not just upon them but upon infidels?

Much as we used to think of Christianity, Muslims still think of Islam. The Islamic teachings they impose upon us might include segregating women from men, or excluding testimony from non-Muslims against Muslims. They will certainly include Islamic blasphemy laws already used in Muslim countries by Muslims bearing grudges against non-Muslims.

The West revoked blasphemy laws when those laws defended Christianity. Immigrant races can impose blasphemy laws defending their religions. Allah commands it.

It is all very well for Western countries to offer sharia to matters between Muslims, but why should sharia not also apply to relations between Muslims and non-Muslims? Subjecting a Muslim to Western laws but not us to sharia would be discriminatory, and we abhor discrimination.

Multiculturalism condemns us to irresolvable conflicts between cultures. At some point, either we assert our cultures in our countries or we capitulate. If we continue to capitulate, Western atheists and agnostics cannot expect to be excused from sharia any more than can Christians of faith.

The Islamisation of the West

In its origins, communism was as hostile to Islam as it was to every other religion. Whatever Marxism came to mean after communism fell in Eastern Europe in 1989 and the Soviet Union collapsed in 1991, it remained a rejection of Western cultures, societies, and civilisation. Replacing Christianity, classic liberalism, and the rest of Western Civilisation with Islam will do.

"I would not want to create the impression that I would not like the government of the United States to be Islamic sometime in the future," said Ibrahim Hooper in 1993. He later became national spokesman for the Council on America–Islamic Relations.

"The Koran...should be the highest authority in America and Islam the only accepted religion on earth," was a reporter's paraphrasing of words that Omar Ahmad, a founder of the Council on America–Islamic Relations, told a conference hall filled with Californian Muslims in 1998.

If Western races do not recover our collective identities and self-belief, which other races never lost, then immigrants will in time prevail over us by the sheer force of their numbers. With or without terror, rapidly changing demographics mean that Western Europe and portions of North America and Australasia will become Muslim.

Other countries and regions formerly Western will not become Muslim only because we succumb to races that are not so ready to succumb to Islam as we are. Those races will determine our future, if we survive.

Our ideological West so assured with multiculturalism and inclusion will not defy any immigrant race or league of races seeking to impose its culture upon us. We will celebrate it.

Polling suggests that something like half of American Muslims want a sharia court system outside the American legal system. Polling also suggests that almost a quarter of American Muslims believe that establishing sharia justifies violent jihad. If they are the figures when there appears to be no chance of that happening, then the prospect of sharia being implemented can only increase its support among races valuing their cultures.

In all events, it is hard to imagine fellow Muslims standing in the way of sharia, although they might dispute between themselves some of the specific requirements. The strictness of sharia for Britain and other formerly Western countries will be for Muslims to decide. Their knowledge and understanding of Islam will prevail, not ours.

Whatever the majority of Muslims thinks hardly matters. Be they races, collective religions, nations, or anything else, tribes are not driven by the majority. The masses are busy with their daily lives: working, feeding their families, or playing. They follow or acquiesce.

Tribes, nations, and races are driven by the few with power and zeal. We are.

No longer the Christian West, there is no reason why we should not be Muslim or anything else not Christian. It would be perfectly natural for the Islamic dream of an Islamic state through North Africa, the Middle East, and western Asia to encompass other lands with large Muslim populations. Suggesting otherwise would be like saying that such a caliphate should not include Turkey, Albania, Bosnia, or Lebanon because those lands once were Christian. Eurabia refers to Europe no longer European blending seamlessly into the Middle East.

Islam becomes Europe's last stand. For a while there, Islamisation of the West or Western countries only appeared in quotation marks, "Islamisation," as if there could never be such a thing.

As we come to welcome the idea, there will be no need to pretend. The West's dogmatic determination not to distinguish between races and religions, except to malign our own, makes our post-Christian Christendom indistinguishable from an Islamic caliphate. So thrilled not to be racist, we find the end of the West exciting.

History is written by the victors. The future will record that Allah, not Jews or Europeans, delivered Europe to Islam.

Our Lands of Other People

Our lands ripe to become lands of other people, we refuse to recognise roles for race or religion. People of other races do not refuse.

Occasionally, word reaches us of Muslims boasting that they are conquering Western countries through immigration. We laugh, fobbing their boasts away, certain that we will remain happily multicultural forever.

Some British police acknowledge consulting with local immigrant leaders before entering immigrant areas, as if that is simply respectful and ought to be normal. Anonymously, they say that those areas are Muslim, although that might be because Muslims are more structured in their societies than other immigrants or because there are so many of them. Muslims are not the only parallel societies amidst multiculturalism.

We refuse to admit reality in respect of religion any more than we admit reality in respect of race. We keep out of other races' areas, without admitting to ourselves that those areas are no longer ours.

Western leaders talk and act as if their role is not to defend our races, countries, and civilisation, but to facilitate the seamless transitions of our countries to becoming other people's countries as smoothly and peacefully as possible. Managing our orderly replacement and succession is our parting gesture before disappearing altogether.

For as long as we give immigrants so much, they have reason to be civil. We do not think so far ahead, but when the pot of gold we provide them exhausts, they will lose that reason to co-operate. They will assert their countries within the countries that we give them.

Then, we might re-engage with reality. We still might not.

Most likely, land that was the West will break along racial lines. People have always divided by tribe and race, until the West began turning against ours.

Even the former Soviet Union allowed different races and ethnic groups their own constituent union republics or autonomous republics within them. In 1987, the last Soviet leader in his support for Africans, Puerto Ricans, and Poles suggested that America should set aside states for each of them.

Pakistani Britain will not merge with North African France, Turkish Germany, or any other post-European country into a single caliphate, because they are of different races, in spite of their shared Muslim faith. Britain will probably partition into Pakistani, Indian, African, and other cities and racial regions, perhaps warring as they forge their boundaries.

Aging Britons from our hidden homes will keep insisting how lovely it all is. We will say we are enriched.

If the second last white person tries to save our race and culture, then in the cry for multiculturalism, the last white person might feel called upon to kill her. We can then finish fighting World War II, but not the war that was.

It took two world wars and a holocaust to bring the West to this point. It might take something similar for us to recover.

We consider any concern about Islam and sharia to be irrational, but break out in hysteria at any hint of fascism. Far from eradicating fascism, we are risking its renewal.

We are laying the groundwork for a future fierce reaction by European peoples casting timidity aside, braver or more desperate than we are now: weak kneed and wimpy. Fascism might prove our only defence from the most extreme sharia, as it has been in Muslim countries.

A return to militarism is not such a risk in nationalist Japan. If Japan remilitarises, it will be for external threats necessitating remilitarisation. Races other than ours do not surrender as meekly as we now do.

Without being a people enjoying self-determination, there is no freedom or other culture, but we must want to be races and want to be nations. We are already races, however much we have forgotten it or wish we could forget it. We can be nations again.

ABOUT THE AUTHOR

Simon Lennon has travelled throughout Europe, America, Australasia, Asia, and the South Pacific, seeing how similar European peoples are to each other (wherever we live) and how different we of the West are to everyone else. He has university bachelor's degrees in science and law and university master's degrees in commerce and business. He is married with six children.

His non-fiction collection *The West* comprises the following sixteen books:

Mending the West
The Unnatural West: An Overview
The Tribeless West: An Overview
The Homeless West: An Overview
The Vanishing West: An Overview

Individualism
Western Individualism
The End of Natural Selection
The Need for Nations

Identity
People's Identity: Race and Racism
Of Whom We're Born: Race and Family
Biological Us: Gender and Sexuality

Nationalism
A Land to Belong: Nationalism
The Failure of Multiculturalism

Cultures
Reclaiming Western Cultures
Christendom Lost
Aiding Islam

He is also the author of another non-fiction book, two collections of short stories, and five novels.

www.ingramcontent.com/pod-product-compliance
Lightning Source LLC
Chambersburg PA
CBHW032138090426
42743CB00029B/733